Samuel French Acting Edition

CW00502927

The Third Story

by Charles Busch

‖ SAMUEL FRENCH ‖

SAMUELFRENCH.COM   **SAMUELFRENCH.CO.UK**

FOR PRODUCTION ENQUIRIES

UNITED STATES AND CANADA
Info@SamuelFrench.com
1-866-598-8449

UNITED KINGDOM AND EUROPE
Plays@SamuelFrench.co.uk
020-7255-4302

Each title is subject to availability from Samuel French, depending upon country of performance. Please be aware that *THE THIRD STORY* may not be licensed by Samuel French in your territory. Professional and amateur producers should contact the nearest Samuel French office or licensing partner to verify availability.

MUSIC USE NOTE

Licensees are solely responsible for obtaining formal written permission from copyright owners to use copyrighted music in the performance of this play and are strongly cautioned to do so. If no such permission is obtained by the licensee, then the licensee must use only original music that the licensee owns and controls. Licensees are solely responsible and liable for all music clearances and shall indemnify the copyright owners of the play(s) and their licensing agent, Samuel French, against any costs, expenses, losses and liabilities arising from the use of music by licensees. Please contact the appropriate music licensing authority in your territory for the rights to any incidental music.

IMPORTANT BILLING AND CREDIT REQUIREMENTS

If you have obtained performance rights to this title, please refer to your licensing agreement for important billing and credit requirements.

THE THIRD STORY was originally commissioned and given its world premiere by the LaJolla Playhouse, La Jolla, California, September 2008 (Christopher Ashley, Artistic Director). The play was directed by Carl Andress. The cast and crew was as follows:

PEG/DR. RUTENSPITZ. . . . . Mary Beth Peil

DREW/STEVE. . . . . Jonathan Walker

QUEENIE BARTLETT/QUEENIE 2/BABA YAGA . . . . Charles Busch

DR. CONSTANCE HUDSON . . . . Jennifer Van Dyck

VERNA/VASALISA . . . . Rebecca Lawrence

ZYGOTE . . . . Scott Parkinson

Original music – Lewis Flynn
Scenic design – David Gallo
Costume design – Gregory Gale
Lighting Design – Christopher Akerlind
Sound Design – Walter Trabach
Wig design – Tom Watson

The New York premiere of **THE THIRD STORY** was produced by MCC Theatre by special arrangement with The Lucille Lortel Theatre Foundation, January 2009 at the Lortel Theatre (Robert LuPone and Bernard Telsey, Artistic Directors, William Cantler, Associate Artistic Director, Blake West, Executive Director). The play was directed by Carl Andress. The cast and crew was as follows:

PEG/DR. RUTENSPITZ. . . . . .Kathleen Turner

DREW/STEVE. . . . . Jonathan Walker

QUEENIE BARTLETT/QUEENIE 2/BABA YAGA . . . . Charles Busch

DR. CONSTANCE HUDSON . . . . Jennifer Van Dyke

VERNA/VASALISA . . . . Sarah Rafferty

ZYGOTE . . . . Scott Parkinson

Original music – Lewis Flynn
Scenic design – David Gallo
Costume design – Gregory Gale
Lighting design – David Weiner
Sound design – Chris Luessmann
Wig design – Tom Watson

CAST OF CHARACTERS
(and suggested doubling of actors)

Actor 1 – **VASALISA/VERNA**

Actor 2 – **BABA YAGA/QUEENIE BARTLETT/QUEENIE 2**

Actor 3 – **PEG/DR. RUTENSPITZ**

Actor 4 – **DREW/STEVE**

Actor 5 – **DR. CONSTANCE HUDSON**

Actor 6 – **ZYGOTE/BABA YAGA DOUBLE**

ACT ONE

Scene One

(Omaha, Nebraska, 1949. Mid-afternoon. A furnished boarding house room, with a worn sofa, an easy chair, a liquor cabinet, a desk with a typewriter and a chair, is currently home to **DREW**, *a young screenwriter and refugee from Hollywood. His mother,* **PEG**, *a veteran screenwriter, is visiting. This room stays throughout the play. All the stories that stem from the minds of Peg and Drew are enacted in this room and among this furniture. Changes of location should be made clear through lighting and sound.)*

*(***DREW*** enters from the kitchen. From offstage, we hear* **PEG** *boisterously talking to him.* **DREW** *lies down on the worn sofa and picks up the book he had been reading.)*

PEG. *(offstage)* I was throwing a million ideas at him. Every kind of story. Comedy, drama, romance.

*(***PEG*** enters from the kitchen. She's a tough, energetic woman in her sixties. She's always been catnip to men, but due to her salty intelligence rather than her beauty.)*

PEG. I'm telling you, this young producer at Republic, his name is M.J. Furman, is a huge fan of mine. The man is on tenterhooks, desperate to read a script, even an outline from the two of us. I promised we'd have something to show him by next week.

DREW. Sorry to disappoint both of you, Mother, but you're looking at a devoted full-time employee of the Post Office. See how great it is? It's Sunday and I have the day off to do nothing but read. Over the next year, I'm thinking of plowing through all of Tolstoy.

PEG. Oh, why couldn't you have been born a fabulous Aries like me? Instead, you're a goddam Pisces. Imaginative and creative but sensitive and easily led astray. We Aries can be exhausting but oh, how brightly we shine. In the game of life, we play to win.

DREW. Well, get used to losing because the answer is still no.

PEG. If you're no longer a writer, why the hell do you have this Smith Corona so prominently displayed? You might as well have a pin spot on it.

DREW. I write letters.

PEG. You don't write me any letters.

DREW. I write to Vera.

PEG. I thought you two broke up.

DREW. She broke up with me. I haven't accepted it yet.

PEG. I never liked that dame. Never trusted her. *(She pours herself a drink.)*

DREW. She hates you too. Vera says you'll never release me from your grasping tentacles.

PEG. Oh really? What other lovely things has she to say about me?

DREW. She says if you expect to find work as a writer again, you're deluding yourself.

PEG. Well, you can tell Vera that if she expects to find work as an actress, she'd better do something about those teeth.

DREW. What's wrong with her teeth?

PEG. Has love blinded you to that overbite? I see no work in her future unless they're casting a hillbilly comedy. Her jealousy knows no bounds.

DREW. Jealous of what? Your dental alignment?

PEG. Jealous of what we share. We have a magic and a chemistry that goes beyond mother and son. She couldn't keep up. She felt excluded. Now I blame her for this whole thing.

DREW. What whole thing?

PEG. Breaking your heart and forcing you into this Midwestern exile in Omaha and a dead-end job as a mailman.

DREW. Mother, you have to accept that I love my job. I love this place. I love my life.

PEG. Forgive me if I remain a skeptic If nothing else, this postal charade is hard on your feet. You always had rotten feet.

DREW. You're the one with the bad feet. Your aristocratic Russian feet that no shoes ever fit. I've got my father's big, wide Midwestern feet.

PEG. Your father has the feet of a murderer.

DREW. I'm impressed. You haven't seen his feet in over thirty years. Perhaps you're confusing my father's feet with those of one of your other five husbands?

PEG. Three husbands, my boy. You keep forgetting I married Miles twice. I was never legally wed to Irwin and my marriage to Jorge was annulled.

DREW. Forgive me. I forgot to bring along my abacus.

PEG. Oh boy, nobody kicks me in the ass like you do. I love it. The banter. The back and forth. Bam, bam, bam. I miss it. I haven't had one good solid laugh since you left.

DREW. Sorry but I'm staying put. I want to get to know my father. And I want to spend time with him before he's too old.

PEG. Well, that's very dear of you. Of course, you know, kid, I'm not enjoying the best of health.

DREW. What's wrong with your health?

PEG. What's wrong with my health? My darling, I was in a major car accident less than three years ago. One never fully recovers from that sort of trauma.

DREW. I don't see any residual effects.

PEG. You refuse to. You like to think of your mother as immortal. Well, she's not. I have many physical problems. I suffer from arthritis. My bones have never fully knit.

DREW. Have you been to a doctor?

PEG. I've had my fill of the medical profession. I've happily returned to my roots as a devout Christian Scientist.

DREW. You're not a devout Christian Scientist.

PEG. Kid, don't tell me what I believe in. Madeleine Andrews and I go once a month to the Christian Science Reading Room.

DREW. I've just never understood how you can be lifelong friends with a pickled-in-vodka ham actress like Madeleine Andrews.

PEG. I'd love to write something for her. The poor thing is starving for a meaty role.

DREW. But she's a terrible actress.

PEG. Explain that to her legion of fans. I can see Madeleine as a very stylish Queen of the mob. The ruthless head of a crime syndicate gowned by Dior. Hey, I bet a raw Freudian-tinged gangster picture would cinch us a deal.

DREW. I don't write as butch as you.

PEG. We make it a woman's picture but with violence instead of violins. We'll give her a troubled son. She adores him and worries how he'll get along after she's gone.

DREW. Digging deep, huh Ma?

PEG. It'll be a picture that speaks to every mother with a difficult child.

Scene Two

(An elegant high rise apartment. **QUEENIE BARTLETT**, *the undisputed first lady of crime, enters. She exists in another world from Peg and Drew; that of a moody film noir crime drama. Onyx hard, she wears only the most elegant and understated of Paris fashions.* **DREW** *puts on a suit jacket and a fedora and plays Queenie's handsome and volatile gangster son,* **STEVE**. *His beautiful, blonde and lethal bride,* **VERNA**, *joins them.)*

QUEENIE. The poor old Ma is always the last to know.

VERNA. I tell you, Mrs. B, there should have been violins playing. Steve says to me, "You think I'm a fibber, huh? You think I'm selling you a bill of goods on this marriage proposal business?"

QUEENIE. Who could resist such a romantic swain?

STEVE. Ma, I tell her to take a gander in the parlor and she sashays in there with a smirk on that beautiful puss of hers and what does she see but a Justice of the Peace.

VERNA. Five minutes later, I emerge Mrs. Steve Bartlett.

QUEENIE. Can't say I'm pleased you denied me the joy of planning your wedding.

STEVE. And what a flash that would have been.

QUEENIE. It would have been the height of elegance. I would have had my couturier Monsieur Andre design Verna's trousseau. The talented frog owes me plenty.

(With lightening dexterity, **STEVE** *jokingly whips a gun out of his pocket.)*

STEVE. Oh yeah? Should we take the boat to France and shake the pansy until his petals fall?

QUEENIE. Darling, please. This penthouse is no place for firearms.

STEVE. Whatever you say, Ma. Whatever you say. *(STEVE puts the gun back in his jacket pocket.)* Ma's pistol packing days are over. She's got others to do the dirty work but once upon a time, my mother handled a machine gun better than Dillinger.

QUEENIE. Well, the invention of the tommy gun was a real blessing. Finally – a machine gun you could carry. Before that, I was one big bruise. When Steve was a kid, he was convinced that the tommy gun was named after some other little boy named Tommy. Oh, he'd pitch a fit. Finally, just to quiet the kid down, I had the fellas call their guns their "Stevie." It got around and soon all the other mobsters thought we'd invented a new weapon. That's what it was like back then. We had fun. Today it's all dollars and cents.

VERNA. Sweet story.

QUEENIE. Verna, it's still not too late for me to take you shopping.

VERNA. It's very kind of you to offer, Mrs. B, and while I certainly admire your legendary chic, I tend to feature a younger look.

QUEENIE. Is that what you call it? Lord, I've never seen so many diamonds worn before noon. And Verna, in this town, summer furs are placed in storage no later than Labor Day.

VERNA. I'll remember that.

STEVE. Doll, maybe you should hold off buying too many clothes, I'll be wanting a son pretty soon. Ma, doesn't Verna look like she could give you plenty of healthy grandkids?

QUEENIE. Son, let's not place the ox before the tart. I'm sorry, a slip of the tongue. I meant the cart. Darling, there's so much I want for you.

STEVE. But I've got so much. I have Verna. Isn't she a beauty?

QUEENIE. Yes, she's quite a hooker. I'm sorry, looker.

STEVE. Another slip of the tongue, Ma?

VERNA. Stevie, we should be going. The train leaves Union Station in less than an hour.

STEVE. Our Palm Springs honeymoon awaits.

VERNA. A train ride into the desert. How can a tough guy like you be afraid to fly?

QUEENIE. He's not afraid of anything.

STEVE. I just don't like being penned in.

QUEENIE. It's a common medical condition called claustrophobia.

STEVE. Aw, Ma. Not now.

QUEENIE. She better know what she's getting into.

VERNA. I like being wise to the score. How long have you had this claustrophobia?

STEVE. All my life. I don't even ride in a car unless the top's down. Get me in a stalled elevator and I'm ready for the bughouse. That's why this great lady here took the rap for me last year. I couldn't face six months in the slammer. How can I ever repay her?

QUEENIE. Son, I needed the rest and was out in time for the fall fashion collections.

VERNA. Guess I'll just have to accept that my tough guy is a Mama's boy. But there's one place where he'll always be mine, unless you've got other ideas, Mrs. Bartlett.

(**QUEENIE** *"accidentally" spills her drink on* **VERNA**'s *dress.* **VERNA** *shrieks.*)

QUEENIE. Oh, Verna. I'm terribly sorry.

VERNA. My dress! She did that on purpose! How am I supposed to get on a train like this?

STEVE. It was an accident, honey. Wasn't it, Ma?

QUEENIE. Of course, it was. Besides, Verna, you ought to know from experience that blood is the only stain that's hard to remove.

VERNA. Steve, are you coming with me, or am I flying to the desert solo?

STEVE. I'm coming with you. I'll phone you, Ma, from the Springs.

(*He kisses her and he and* **VERNA** *exit.* **QUEENIE** *remains very perturbed.* **STEVE** *removes his jacket and hat and returns to being* **DREW**.)

Scene Three

(Omaha. The living room. We continue where we left off.)

PEG. Now watch it, honey. Let's not make the mob queen a horrible bitch. We're writing this for Madeleine. She's not some sweaty, legs over her head B-movie actress.

DREW. Mother, I'm not working on this movie with you. And hey, I write great roles for women.

PEG. I beg to differ. Lately, you're always making your lead female character a selfish, unsympathetic harridan.

DREW. Not true. How can you say that?

PEG. You did it with the magazine editor in your last picture. You even did it with the manicurist in that dreadful comedy you worked on at Fox.

DREW. Dreadful? You told me you screamed with laughter.

PEG. I was being a devoted mother and downed a fifth of scotch.

DREW. Well, you don't need me. You've never written with a partner.

PEG. I need you now. I've hesitated bringing this up, darling, but perhaps I should prepare you. I could be under investigation from the House Un-American Activities Committee.

DREW. Have you received a summons to appear in Washington?

PEG. Not yet, but I have enemies who would gladly finger me.

DREW. Do you have anything in your past, besides slugging Ginger Rogers, which could get you in trouble?

PEG. When I was married to Miles, he made me sign all sorts of petitions to defeat Franco in Spain. I may have joined the goddam Communist Party and not even known it. I tell you, any moment someone out there is gonna finger me.

DREW. Mother, would you please stop using that phrase?

PEG. I could very well be blacklisted. If we collaborate, I may need you to take a solo credit. I can't imagine life without work. I've been making up stories my entire life.

DREW. You certainly have.

PEG. I recall you being quite enraptured with my narrative abilities when you were a child.

DREW. I loved your stories. You had an endless collection of Russian fairy tales.

PEG. The stories my Grandmother Olga told me.

DREW. I liked the one about the firebird and the woebegone Princess.

(The beautiful but painfully shy **PRINCESS VASALISA** *runs on in her Russian fairy tale.)*

PEG. What was her name? Vasalisa?

DREW. Yeah. Vasalisa.

Scene Three B

(The fairy tale past. Nightfall. A small hut deep within a Russian forest. **VASALISA** *searches for an inhabitant of the hut.)*

VASALISA. Baba Yaga? Baba Yaga?

(The **BABA YAGA** *emerges. She is an old witch, swathed in rags and shadows.)*

BABA YAGA. Princess Vasalisa, you are here at long last.

VASALISA. You- you know my – my name?

BABA YAGA. I was expecting you. The lair of the Baba Yaga is everyone's greatest fear and last hope. There are many questions you long to ask. Is it true I feed off the blood of stray cats? Am I guilty of strangling my daughter with her own braid? Did I indeed poison my late husband's kugel?

VASALISA. Well, di - did you?

BABA YAGA. I ANSWER NOTHING! Now tell me, child, what brings you to the forest.

VASALISA. I – I – it is so diffi –impossi – if you only –

(The **BABA YAGA** *hands her a bladder full of wine that was hanging from her shoulder.)*

BABA YAGA. Child, take a sip of this fine kvass. It will loosen your tongue. It was given to me by Smigel the wine merchant, for turning his straying son-in-law into a woodpecker.

*(***VASALISA** *drinks from the bladder.)*

VASALISA. I'm afraid, I am not ac-accu-accust – *(The wine takes effect and suddenly she's remarkably articulate.)* Oh my. I feel a hitherto unknown ease of verbal acuity. Baba Yaga, I am so utterly and miserably in love with Prince Mishka. He is everything one could wish for in a husband. But why would he want me? I should only prove an embarrassment and burden to any man. Please, Baba Yaga, please make him love me. There must be something I can give you. Gold? I have gold.

(She rummages through her small change purse. She takes out a golden feather.)

BABA YAGA. What have you there?

VASALISA. Oh this? A feather that dropped from the sky.

*(**VASALISA** hands it to her.)*

BABA YAGA. A feather bright as flame. It fell from the breast of the enchanted firebird. It sheds its feathers on a blessed few.

VASALISA. Then you shall make it possible for the Prince to fall in love with me?

BABA YAGA. We shall make of you a twin; someone who is everything you are but more. She shall captivate the Prince in your stead. After he proposes marriage to this double, all you need do is wish it and she will quickly and painlessly die.

VASALISA. How, may I ask, do we create this twin?

BABA YAGA. Shortly, I shall take a hatchet and cleave you in two. You will of course, feel nothing. One hopes. The rest of the spell I shall explain to you later. Now come, child, we have much to do. Come!

*(The **BABA YAGA** pulls **VASALISA** off into the hut.)*

Scene Three C

(Omaha. The scene continues.)

DREW. At the end, Princess Vasalisa climbs on the back of an enchanted firebird and flies off gloriously alone and independent into the sunset.

PEG. Your favorite story, huh? Dr. Freud would say you wanted to escape from me. I always thought it was the two of us against the world. All the men in my life, all my husbands, were mere side shows and they damn well knew it. That knowledge at times earned me a bloodied lip, a blackened eye and a punch in the stomach.

DREW. I seem to recall you giving as good as you got.

PEG. My pet, a woman of achievement; be it in business, the arts, politics or science, is truly the most vulnerable of God's creatures. Science. Hey, how about a science fiction yarn? Since Uncle Sam put Nagasaki in the pressure cooker, they're all the rage.

DREW. I don't know anything about science.

PEG. What's to know? Toss in some fifty-cent words like homo sapien and protozoa. Make it about a glamorous lady scientist who's on the cusp of a breakthrough that could benefit or destroy mankind. A perfect role for Linda Belmont. She's under contract to Republic. Linda looks like she could possibly spell "molecule."

Scene Four

(A scientific laboratory. **DREW** *remains lying on the sofa.* **DR. CONSTANCE HUDSON** *enters, carrying a clipboard. She exists in a different story from Peg and Drew; a B-movie science fiction picture. A beautiful woman, she masks her vulnerability with a severe upswept hairdo and an intimidating air of efficiency.)*

CONSTANCE. Dr. Rutenspitz!

(PEG dons a pair of glasses and a German accent and becomes **DR. RUTENSPITZ.***)*

DR. RUTENSPITZ. Yes, dear Constance. What is it you could not discuss on the telephone?

CONSTANCE. The Rappaport Foundation has decided not to renew my research grant.

DR. RUTENSPITZ. Oh, no, my dear.

CONSTANCE. In their infinite wisdom, they have chosen to lend their financial support to Dr. Meinhardt Biederman. I have nothing but contempt for these petty administrators with their paltry little dreams.

DR. RUTENSPITZ. Your field of study frightens them. Creating a duplicate human being questions the very essence of mankind.

CONSTANCE. I cannot concern myself with trifles. I offer up this question. Is mankind worthy of our intelligence? You possess the most fertile mind since Galileo and yet you've been metaphorically castrated by the scientific community.

DR. RUTENSPITZ. How ironic since for years I've been accused of having penis envy. My dear Constance, I have at times lamented never marrying, never having a child. Will you one day regret your personal sacrifice to science?

CONSTANCE. I've had my share of romantic folderol. Leaves one physically exhausted, mentally befogged and unprepared to conduct accurate diagnostic research.

DR. RUTENSPITZ. My child, have you never been in love?

CONSTANCE. Dr. R, are you hoping to uncover the secret wound responsible for my frosty exterior?

DR. RUTENSPITZ. Was there someone in the past that hurt you?

CONSTANCE. Let me ponder that. Have I ever felt abandoned? Was there an episode in my life where I fell head over heels in love, desperately and completely, so much so that I would have gladly given my life for his happiness? And then been tossed aside, left disconsolate and stripped of all hope? No. Can't say I have. Dr. Rutenspitz, I have no fear of ending up a spinster academic with a test tube full of sperm. In fact, I welcome it.

DR. RUTENSPITZ. If you will excuse me, dear Constance, I am on tenterhooks to complete my liver enzyme protocol.

CONSTANCE. The good work must continue.

*(**DR. R.** exits. Unbeknownst to **CONSTANCE,** **ZYGOTE,** an ageless male being, eerily beautiful yet grotesque, has snuck into the lab and is standing behind her.)*

ZYGOTE. Dr. Hudson.

CONSTANCE. Zygote!

ZYGOTE. Did I frighten you? I hope so.

CONSTANCE. No. Merely startled.

ZYGOTE. Nothing can keep me away from you.

CONSTANCE. I like to think that you can always regard this laboratory as home.

ZYGOTE. I should. It's the place of my birth. But then we can't really call it a birth, can we?

CONSTANCE. For me, it was a most profound moment.

ZYGOTE. Really? I'd consider myself one of your most egregious failures.

CONSTANCE. Not at all. I'm very proud of you, Zygote. You were an invaluable stepping-stone to my ultimate clinical conclusions. For that I shall always be grateful.

ZYGOTE. That's a good one. Grateful to a botched experiment.

CONSTANCE. Botched? Why you're a great success. You live, you breathe, you walk, you talk. If you feel unattractive, reserve your anger for your tailor. I can't say I'm mad for that jacket.

ZYGOTE. I'm a tough fit. Perhaps it's that pesky seventh nipple. In the past two years since you granted me my independence, I've had forty-three wisdom teeth extracted and six appendectomies. And then of course, there's my very original intestinal tract.

CONSTANCE. Well, I for one thought we were awfully clever in creating an alternate opening for waste elimination.

ZYGOTE. Yes, *very* clever. Because of that ingenious new opening, I now have to wear a TOUPEE! YOU MAD-WOMAN! WHAT HAVE YOU DONE TO ME?

CONSTANCE. I will not take such abuse from a –

ZYGOTE. From a what? From a lab experiment? The brilliant Dr. Hudson did her brilliant best creating life in a test tube and then tried out her new method to mature the Zygote to full adulthood in a matter of hours. Gosh darn, it's working. No, wait a minute. There's something wrong. Something hideously wrong. Destroy it. Put it out of its misery.

CONSTANCE. That's not how it was.

ZYGOTE. My earliest memory is hearing frightened voices shouting, "Kill it, kill it!"

CONSTANCE. Yes, "kill it," they said. "Kill it." That much is true. I refused to let you die.

ZYGOTE. Why? What did I mean to you?

CONSTANCE. You meant – my life's work. Hours of intense study and labor. So much had built to that moment.

ZYGOTE. It only meant something to you professionally? I grew up virtually alone with you in this lab. Don't you recognize yourself? The way I talk? The words I choose? You know, I perform a very cruel and accurate impersonation of you. It's quite a hit in scientific circles. Does that make you angry?

CONSTANCE. I have more important things with which to concern myself.

ZYGOTE. You know, it's possible that you're more of a zombie than I am.

CONSTANCE. You've succeeded in insulting me. Have you come for more than merely settling old scores?

ZYGOTE. You know what I came for. Give it to me!

CONSTANCE. I will not encourage you in your addictions.

ZYGOTE. My addictions? My one addiction is to your patented chemical SP 596.

CONSTANCE. Abuse of this compound could lead to serious destruction of the nervous system.

ZYGOTE. Give it to me. It's the same chemical that made me age thirty years in three hours. Now, I need it to live.

CONSTANCE. You do not need it to live. That is a falsehood.

ZYGOTE. I do need it. Every atom in my body craves it.

CONSTANCE. Zygote, you place me in a dreadful quandary.

ZYGOTE. I'm begging you, Dr. Hudson. You owe me this much.

CONSTANCE. Oh, all right. Just this once. *(She prepares the injection.)*

ZYGOTE. Thank you. May I inquire; are you any closer to creating your perfect human double?

CONSTANCE. Quite close.

ZYGOTE. You must be working around the clock. No time for friends?

CONSTANCE. I'm afraid not. I had hoped that *you* would make friends.

ZYGOTE. I find the general population as repulsive as they find me.

CONSTANCE. I too prefer my own company.

ZYGOTE. We're cut from the same cloth, eh?

CONSTANCE. You look thin. Have you been eating?

ZYGOTE. I take my meals at the boarding house. I don't seem to be gaining any weight. I suspect the fat German cook sucks all the nutrients out of the meat before she serves it.

CONSTANCE. You really do an impersonation of me?

ZYGOTE. Oscar worthy.

CONSTANCE. Hold still. *(She gives him the injection.)*

ZYGOTE. Ahhhh. The chemical. It's instant. I keep forgetting that. Ahhh. You're the crazy genius of all time. You gotta market this thing. It's a killer.

CONSTANCE. I have no intention of being in the business of trafficking illegal substances. And neither should you.

ZYGOTE. What's that supposed to mean?

CONSTANCE. It's no secret that selling morphine is your stock in trade.

ZYGOTE. So what if it is? We all have to earn a living. And we all need our crutch.

CONSTANCE. What am I to do with you?

ZYGOTE. You'd like to see me destroyed. Wouldn't you? Thrown in the garbage with the rest of the medical refuse. Well, I'm not going anywhere, Dr. Hudson. You and I are linked together forever or until I decide to bring you down. And I will bring you down. I'll bring down this entire building.

(He runs out of the lab and crosses into Queenie's Penthouse.)

Scene Five

(Queenie's Penthouse. **QUEENIE** *enters.* **ZYGOTE** *is waiting for her. She takes a wad of money out of her purse.)*

QUEENIE. Same price?

ZYGOTE. For you, Mrs. Bartlett, the price never changes.

QUEENIE. You should be doing pretty good in this racket. Maybe it's time you spent some money on your appearance.

ZYGOTE. There's not enough money in the world that can help me.

QUEENIE. Kid, pardon me for asking but what in heaven's name happened to you?

ZYGOTE. A simple explanation. I'm a medical experiment gone wrong. But I've been told that I should derive satisfaction from the fact that my handicap will ultimately serve mankind.

QUEENIE. I'm not following you.

ZYGOTE. I was created in a lab. A bold step into the future. My creator, the estimable Dr. Constance Hudson, is on the threshold of conceiving a perfect double for any living creature.

QUEENIE. A double?

ZYGOTE. A complete duplication molecule by molecule of one organism for another.

QUEENIE. She knows how to make a twin?

ZYGOTE. She's working on it. But like everyone else, she needs cash.

QUEENIE. I got cash.

ZYGOTE. As well as a cancer in your body that's killing you.

QUEENIE. How do you figure that?

ZYGOTE. I was created with keen powers of deduction. The morphine helps the pain.

QUEENIE. I need to stick around a while longer. I have a kid who needs me.

ZYGOTE. Steve Bartlett seems like a pretty tough customer. I hear he makes grown men cry.

QUEENIE. We've got an angry Senator on our backs. Crenshaw's committed to wiping scum like us off the face of the earth. I'm not worth much but my boy is. This Crenshaw business requires a finesse that doesn't come easy to Steve. It's about negotiation and giving them a piece of the action. That's why I've lasted so long in this line of work. So this doctor can really make you a twin?

ZYGOTE. If anybody could.

(QUEENIE smiles to herself.)

ZYGOTE. Penny for your thoughts, Mrs. Bartlett.

QUEENIE. Oh, I was remembering a fairy tale I heard as a girl. I grew up in an orphan asylum that made San Quentin seem like the Ritz. But there was one matron who had a soft spot for me. Awfully quaint I should think of that now.

ZYGOTE. Tell me more. I grew up in a laboratory. No one ever told me such a story.

(PRINCESS VASALISA runs through the forest.)

QUEENIE. Believe it or not, I was a painfully meek young thing. This matron told me a story about a very shy Princess who was madly in love with a handsome Prince. There was no way this fella would ever wink at her, let alone slip a ring on her finger. So she visits a kindly old woman in the forest, who makes her an identical twin with a gift for gab, and gives the Princess the future she'd considered hopeless. I need some strong magic now, kid. Can you arrange for me to meet this Dr. Hudson?

ZYGOTE. I believe that's within my powers.

QUEENIE. You'd have my eternal appreciation.

(She goes to shake his hand and instead surprisingly hugs him. He's taken aback.)

QUEENIE. What's wrong? Did I hurt you? You don't have fins back there, do you?

ZYGOTE. I wouldn't touch me if I didn't have to.

QUEENIE. Everyone deserves to be touched. You and I are in the same boat, aren't we? Time is running out for you too.

ZYGOTE. Excellent deduction, Mrs. B. I was designed only to last a decade. I've never expected more.

QUEENIE. Oh honey, I expected so much more.

Scene Six

(The Laboratory. **QUEENIE,** *picking up a fur stole, is looking over the place.)*

CONSTANCE. Your offer is extraordinary. But you understand, there can be no strings attached.

QUEENIE. Dr. Hudson, my only goal is for you to succeed. Losing your funding was a rotten break.

CONSTANCE. The scientific bureaucracy has effectively neutralized my attempts to create life from life.

QUEENIE. Well, your dark days are over. Whatever you need, I'll foot the bill. The double, the identical twin. It shows up full size? The same age as the original?

CONSTANCE. That is what I am attempting to do. Yes.

QUEENIE. But can you stuff the brain with all the memories of the original person?

CONSTANCE. I am of the belief that memory is connected to cellular structure.

QUEENIE. What about the sense of humor? Would the double have to be a grim-faced Gussie?

CONSTANCE. Wit can be viewed as a by-product of cerebral configuration.

QUEENIE. What about love? Can you transfer feelings from one person to another?

CONSTANCE. Mrs. Bartlett, are you by chance hoping I would make a double of you?

QUEENIE. That's the ticket.

CONSTANCE. You are intrigued by the fantasy of being in two places at once?

QUEENIE. Yes. Because one of us will be lying in a grave. I'm dying, Dr. Hudson. I need this double to carry on my work and to protect my son.

CONSTANCE. Your work is not unfamiliar to me. I've read about "the Bartlett Syndicate" in connection with Senator Crenshaw's investigation of organized crime.

QUEENIE. Don't believe everything you read in the papers. Sure, I walk on the shady side of the street from time to time, but no more than any of the folks you vote for on Election Day. One more question. If this double is exactly like me, wouldn't it also have the same tumor?

CONSTANCE. I shouldn't think so. But there would be that risk. However, you seem like a woman who thrives on risk.

QUEENIE. When do we get started?

CONSTANCE. My work has never ended. Despite my financial woes, I've maintained a skeleton staff.

QUEENIE. I meant, when do you make my twin?

CONSTANCE. I'm still doing clinical trials on rodents. I will not be rushed. My credo has always been "Collect, collate, evaluate."

QUEENIE. Evaluate this, Dr. Hudson. I'm a dame on borrowed time.

CONSTANCE. Well, Mrs. Bartlett, I'll certainly pursue this avenue of thinking and get back to you.

QUEENIE. Lady, you beat the band.

CONSTANCE. I beg your pardon.

QUEENIE. You're in no position to turn up your fine schnozzola at my offer. I've done my research as well. You owe months of back rent on this shabby piece of real estate. In fact, at the end of this month, you're going to be tossed out on your biological keister. I'll have my lawyers draw up the papers and you'll find me at Bullocks shopping for a fashionable new wardrobe for my twin. Good day, Dr. Hudson.

(QUEENIE *exits, followed by* CONSTANCE.)

Scene Seven

(Omaha. **PEG** *and* **DREW** *enter from the kitchen.)*

PEG. So the lady scientist and the mob queen make some kind of pact. What's next?

DREW. I haaaate this story. First it was a gangster film. Then it was a science fiction picture. Now, we're scrambling the two together?

PEG. As I get older, I find I have two false starts for every script. It's that third story that finally takes off.

DREW. If I was going to write a movie, it would be a love story. A tragic love story to suit my current romantic situation.

PEG. If you're referring to Vera, that buck toothed broad was no Juliet.

DREW. She was a great girl. You did everything short of murder to break us up. I know about the letter you wrote her. I know about your "just us girls" lunch at the Formosa.

PEG. It was agonizing watching her dominate you.

DREW. You see no irony in that statement? None of my girl-friends have passed the test. None of my friends were good enough. Every kid I brought around was either a nitwit or "Hollywood peasantry."

PEG. Why should my opinion mean so much? You could have rebelled. I have great respect for rebels.

DREW. Living in Omaha is my act of rebellion.

PEG. Drew, perhaps I was wrong keeping us so isolated. I did have the girls around to liven things up.

DREW. Your pals from the silent days. Not much fun for a ten year-old.

PEG. You wanna write a love story? Fine. Let's write a love story. I'm great with love scenes.

DREW. You write great prison riots. You write great elephant stampedes. Love scenes? No. And it makes sense. Despite the multitude of men in your life, you've never loved any of them. You love your work.

PEG. I love you.

DREW. I want to write something where the lovers never speak of love. I want to explore hidden desires which the characters are afraid to reveal. .

PEG. Well, let's not make their desires too hidden. At some point the leading man better metaphorically haul out his pecker.

(**PEG** *remains seated on the sofa.* **DREW** *once more puts on his jacket and hat and becomes* **STEVE**.)

Scene Eight

(Queenie's Office. **STEVE** *rests against the desk.* **CONSTANCE** *looks around.)*

CONSTANCE. Mrs. Bartlett must be commended on her exquisite taste in decor. I've never seen an office with such flair.

STEVE. Ma's a sucker for anything Louis Quinze. What do you think of this cologne she brought over from gay Paree? Does it do anything for me? *(He brings his wrist to her nose.)*

CONSTANCE. The salt in your epidermis is over-activating the Isopropyl Butanol in the toilet water.

STEVE. Gee, I better haul myself over to a Turkish Bath and sweat this thing off. Nothing I like better than sitting in the raw with my buddies and having a good steam. You should try it some time.

CONSTANCE. I'll take that under advisement. I came here to see your mother.

STEVE. Regretfully, Ma's not available. Anything I can do?

CONSTANCE. I received a very nasty letter this morning from my landlord, Mr. McMullin. He's threatening to put a padlock on the laboratory doors for non-payment of rent.

STEVE. Ah, you shouldn't have gotten that letter. It's old news. Mother's motto has always been "eliminate the middle man," so she decided to buy the whole building from McMullin. We are now the proud owners of the newly christened Bartlett Center for Scientific Research.

CONSTANCE. How extraordinary.

STEVE. Dr. Hudson, you could use a little renovating as well. It doesn't take an expert to see that the basic structure is sound.

CONSTANCE. I'm afraid your mother didn't teach you manners. Now if you will excuse me, I have plasma that needs thawing.

STEVE. I still don't see why you and Ma wanna go around making doubles of people, but I guess I'm not an advanced thinker like the two of youse.

CONSTANCE. Your mother possesses a vision of tomorrow that very few share.

STEVE. If we'd been in business with you earlier, you wouldn't have lost that research grant.

CONSTANCE. Mr. Bartlett, I hardly see what influence you could have had with the Rappaport Foundation.

STEVE. That Professor who got the prize instead of you. Dr. Meinhardt Biederman. Things haven't quite worked out for him lately.

CONSTANCE. He received one of the largest financial grants the scientific community has to offer.

STEVE. It's been rescinded. Dr. Biederman was arrested last week for inappropriate relations with an underage girl. The Judge didn't take kindly to the key evidence; a portfolio of highly incriminating photos.

CONSTANCE. I don't believe it.

STEVE. Thought you'd be pleased.

CONSTANCE. I take no pleasure from Dr. Biederman's disgrace. I'm deeply distressed. That poor young girl.

STEVE. Don't worry. There was no young girl.

CONSTANCE. I don't understand.

STEVE. Dr. Biederman was indeed photographed by a hidden shutterbug in the privacy of his home but with his own hatchet-faced middle-aged spouse. Through the aid of trick photography, her photo was replaced with that of a very youthful adult circus midget.

CONSTANCE. You? You did this? You ruined an innocent man?

STEVE. He stole your big chance.

CONSTANCE. Did your Mother know about this?

STEVE. Know about it? She bought the dress for the midget. She went to a lot of trouble. You might want to thank her.

CONSTANCE. This is appalling. I must end this association at once.

STEVE. Ah, calm down, sister. You're sitting in clover. Ma's crazy about you and your work and you know she has deep pockets.

CONSTANCE. I can only imagine where that money comes from. Your mother lied to me. She said the accusations from the Senate investigation were unsubstantiated.

STEVE. No one calls my mother a liar. No one.

CONSTANCE. I have no doubt that lying is the least of her crimes.

STEVE. Who do you think you're fooling? You got into this outfit with your eyes open and you'll go out with your eyes open, only there'll be pennies on 'em.' If you have important work to do in your laboratory, I suggest you do it. Now get out of here.

(PEG *puts on her glasses and once more becomes* DR. RUTENSPITZ.)

Scene Nine

(The Laboratory. **CONSTANCE** *is dictating a letter to* **DR. RUTENSPITZ**.*)*

CONSTANCE. "Mrs. Bartlett, I shall forever condemn myself for believing that a woman of your reputation could ever enter into an honest partnership." How is that for clarity?

DR. RUTENSPITZ. One could question the sentence structure but the message is quite clear.

CONSTANCE. Dr. Rutenspitz, you do see that I have no choice. The woman is devoid of scruples.

DR. RUTENSPITZ. Of course, you cannot be associated with an underworld figure. But one might fear some form of retaliation.

CONSTANCE. Take this down. "I have been notified by the Rappaport Foundation that the grant given to Dr. Biederman has now, due to his unfortunate scandal, been offered to me.

Scene Ten

(Queenie's Office. **STEVE** *is reading the letter aloud to* **QUEENIE, VERNA** *and* **ZYGOTE**.*)*

STEVE. "I, of course, will accept their generous financial assistance while doing everything in my power to restore my colleague's good name." Notice she's still pocketing the dough.

VERNA. I've never known a dame yet who'd sneer at a full purse.

QUEENIE. Keep reading.

STEVE. "I have already moved my equipment and files out of the building that you undoubtedly stole from Mr. McMullin, and into a new laboratory provided by the Rappaport Foundation."

ZYGOTE. I'll provide her with something she won't forget.

STEVE. "Thus, Mrs. Bartlett, concludes an ugly chapter in scientific research."

ZYGOTE. I'll give her a conclusion.

STEVE. "Regretfully yours, Dr. Constance Hudson."

ZYGOTE. She'll regret it all right.

STEVE. Well, Ma, we got bigger fish to fry. By next Friday, we're gonna have control of half the ports in this country. We've got our judges exactly where we want 'em. Senator Crenshaw and his cronies can't lay a finger on us.

QUEENIE. And after all I've done for this country. How many times have they asked me to rub out a foreign agent? And I did it free of charge. Didn't even bill 'em for expenses. In '39, I offered to assassinate Hitler. I had a window of opportunity and could have saved countless lives, but the feds suddenly felt my hands weren't clean enough for the job. They can call me a sociopath and a parasite but nobody can say I'm not a good American.

STEVE. I wouldn't let that committee ruffle your ruffles. When I'm finished, the gentleman's title will be the late Senator Crenshaw.

QUEENIE. Don't say that, Steve. Don't even kid about it.

STEVE. Leave it to me, Ma.

QUEENIE. No, son. Believe me; I'd also like to see him booked into the funeral parlor. And there are plenty others I'd like to see lying on a slab. *(She shoots a glance at* VERNA.*)* But only in my heart. My head tells me different and in our business, we can't be led by our hearts.

STEVE. All right, Ma. For you I'll grant both him and the lady scientist a reprieve.

VERNA. Frankly, Mother Bartlett, this whole *double* notion gave me the willies. I always thought you were tossing away good money. There's only one of me and that's the way my fella likes it.

*(*QUEENIE *slaps her across the face.)*

STEVE. Ma, why'd you do that for?

QUEENIE. Forgive me, Verna.

VERNA. You're gonna let her get away with this?

STEVE. Ma's upset. She's taking this hard.

VERNA. I've put up with plenty. Mrs. Bartlett, from day one you've never liked me.

QUEENIE. No, I don't like you, Verna. I don't like anything about you.

STEVE. Ma, don't say that. You're talking to my wife.

QUEENIE. That's our misfortune. I don't trust you, Verna. I know what dogs you've lain with and I know you're still wagging your tail for them.

VERNA. You've got nothing on me. You'd put the hex on any dame who came between you and your precious little boy.

STEVE. Shut your trap, Verna.

(He slaps her.)

VERNA. Can't you see it? She wants you for herself. An angel from Heaven wouldn't be good enough. She'd dig and find some long-forgotten secret to spoil it for you.

QUEENIE. Enough, Verna!

(**QUEENIE** *slaps her.*)

VERNA. She doesn't want you to be with another woman. She's greedy.

STEVE. I said, enough!

(**STEVE** *slaps her again.*)

VERNA. She'll suck the riches out of this entire city, this entire country and it'll never be enough. And you, Steve, no matter how much love you give her, she'll always want more.

(**QUEENIE** *slaps her again.*)

STEVE. Ma, you have no right to do that to her.

QUEENIE. I have every right.

VERNA. You're gonna have to choose, Steve.

QUEENIE. Do you hear me asking that?

STEVE. Stop it! Stop it! The both of you!

(**STEVE** *slaps* **VERNA.**)

QUEENIE. Let her go, son. You can find better.

STEVE. Maybe I'm not so greedy. This one's enough for me.

QUEENIE. Then you're askin' for nothin'.

STEVE. Verna's right. Any girl of mine is your sworn enemy. Goodbye, Ma.

(**STEVE** *and* **VERNA** *exit.* **QUEENIE** *has forgotten that* **ZYGOTE** *is there. She starts to cry.*)

ZYGOTE. Don't let them get to you, Mrs. Bartlett. You're worth more than all of them.

QUEENIE. *(She rips up the letter.)* Damn her! Damn her!

ZYGOTE. He'll be back. That tramp will be old news before the early edition comes out.

QUEENIE. I could care less about Verna. It's the noble Dr. Hudson who should be damned to Hell. So full of moral indignation. So full of integrity. Oh, she's just busting with it!

(**PEG** *and* **DREW** *appear in their Omaha world.*)

PEG. All right. Enough play acting. I found it.

DREW. The severed head in the refrigerator?

ZYGOTE. You gonna kill her?

QUEENIE. You've seen too many motion pictures.

DREW. What exactly did you find, Mother?

QUEENIE. If we can't have the good doctor, we shall have her formula.

PEG. While you were out on your postal rounds, I was snooping around your room.

ZYGOTE. Might I be of help?

PEG. I do my own leg work.

QUEENIE. I do my own leg work but there are times when it's necessary to pull off "an inside job."

(**QUEENIE** *and* **ZYGOTE** *exit.*)

Scene Thirteen

(Omaha, the living room. We continue where we left off.)

PEG. I stumbled upon your manuscript. Your new play.

DREW. It's not a new play. It's something that I worked on a long time ago and is now consigned to the bottom of my sock drawer.

PEG. It is a new play and a good one. I think it's brilliant.

DREW. Really?

PEG. It goes far beyond anything I could have written.

DREW. Come on.

PEG. A hundred per cent on the level. I think it's kind of a crazy masterpiece. Drew, I can't tell you how pleased I am that you're writing. It pained me to think you'd given it up.

DREW. I gave up screen writing for hire. Not writing. I've been re-reading the early novels of Dostoyevsky. I was trying to give it an element of the comic grotesque.

PEG. You achieved a wonderful balance. In a moment, I'm going to toss out the word, genius.

DREW. I can't believe you liked it so much. Wow. And the part where the mother slaps the girlfriend? Too much?

PEG. Loved that she slapped her several times.

(CONSTANCE enters, excitedly studying a twenty-foot long print-out of data.)

PEG. Brilliant! That's all I can say.

CONSTANCE. It is, isn't it?

DREW. Really? Honestly?

PEG. Right hand to God.

Scene Twelve

(*The Laboratory. A week later.* **PEG** *once more becomes* **DR. RUTENSPITZ**. **DREW** *remains on the sofa.* **CONSTANCE** *and* **DR. RUTENSPITZ** *continue their study of the print-out.*)

CONSTANCE. Months of diligent hard work have paid off.

DR. RUTENSPITZ. With this data, you can truly begin. Will you contact the scientific journals?

CONSTANCE. Oh no. I am far from ready to disclose my findings. But mark my words, within two years – nay, sixteen months, I shall successfully create a human double in this laboratory.

DR. RUTENZPITZ. You will have gone beyond anything I have ever achieved.

(**DREW** *puts on his fedora and joins them as* **STEVE**, *carrying a small package.*)

STEVE. Good afternoon, ladies.

CONSTANCE. How did you get past the locked doors?

STEVE. It doesn't require a PhD. Won't you introduce me to your esteemed colleague?

CONSTANCE. This is Dr. Rutenspitz. Mr. Stephen Bartlett.

DR. RUTENSPITZ. Oh, the uh –

STEVE. That's right. The son of.

CONSTANCE. Mr. Bartlett, what can I do for you?

STEVE. You left something behind in your mad haste to escape our dastardly clutches. (*She reaches for the package.*) I'd rather you opened it when we were alone.

CONSTANCE. You are impertinent.

DR. RUTENSPITZ. Dr. Hudson, I can leave the room.

STEVE. You're my kind of gal, Doc. Quick on the draw.

DR. RUTENSPITZ. Constance, I shall see you tomorrow. And, my dear, get some rest. Good day, Mr. Bartlett.

(*She exits the scene, and returns to being* **PEG** *and to her chair in the living room.*)

STEVE. Been burning the late night oil?

CONSTANCE. And if I have?

STEVE. It becomes you. Your hair isn't quite so – tight.

CONSTANCE. Now may I see what's inside that package?

STEVE. My pleasure.

(**STEVE** *hands her the package. She unwraps it. It's a pair of bedroom slippers.*)

STEVE. They were found in a closet in the old lab. You didn't miss 'em? They look awfully comfy.

CONSTANCE. It was thoughtful of you to return them. Why? I should think I would be persona non grata in the world of Queenie Bartlett and company.

STEVE. You're not on her list of favorites. That was not a nice letter you wrote her. Hurt her feelings. Hurt 'em bad.

CONSTANCE. It was an unfortunate situation I prefer not to discuss. How is your mother?

STEVE. Something's up with her. I don't think she's well. Of course, she denies it. I told her she should see a doctor. Maybe she's anemic.

CONSTANCE. Is that why you're here? You think I know something?

STEVE. Do you? My mother's everything in the world to me.

CONSTANCE. There's really nothing I can tell you.

STEVE. You seem different today.

CONSTANCE. We've had some exciting developments.

STEVE. That's good. *(pause)* When things go well, gets you charged up. What's that chemical inside that makes your heart race?

CONSTANCE. Adrenaline.

STEVE. Yeah. Adrenaline.

CONSTANCE. I really must get back to work.

STEVE. That great brain of yours is always charged.

CONSTANCE. Sometimes I don't know what to think.

(He takes her in his arms and kisses her.)

CONSTANCE. Oh, Stephen, please. I'm not the sort of woman who – *(She yields to his kisses.)*

STEVE. You're not thinking now.

(He kisses her again passionately. She pulls away.)

CONSTANCE. Stephen, I can't help but wonder if I'm not merely a feminine symbol that you're compelled to penetrate for social rather than sexual gratification.

STEVE. Nope. I've got the plain, old-fashioned hots for you.

(He grabs her close to him and kisses her again. Once more, **CONSTANCE** *pulls away.)*

CONSTANCE. This is wrong, Stephen. You have a wife.

STEVE. Let's have this moment to remember.

CONSTANCE. Would that be enough for you? Wouldn't you want more?

STEVE. You're very confident. I like that in a woman.

CONSTANCE. What you mistake for confidence is merely an old maid's trepidation of the phallus.

STEVE. Connie, I wouldn't do anything to hurt you.

CONSTANCE. I'm afraid my studies of the male of the species have left me singularly unimpressed.

STEVE. Angel, there's an old saying I once read in a book, and truer words were never written. *(He caresses her cheek.)* "Don't, by all means don't, believe everything you read in books."

(Steve tips his hat and exits, leaving **CONNIE** *breathless.)*

Scene Thirteen

(The Fairy Tale Past. The **BABA YAGA** *leads* **VASALISA**
through the forest.)

BABA YAGA. Come, child. Do not straggle behind. The field
of blackberries is just ahead.

VASALISA. Yes, Ba-Baba Yaga.

(She sees a rat and shrieks.)

BABA YAGA. It is only a rat. Formerly the Inn Keeper, Yakov
Petrovitch. He'll no longer turn away a hungry trav-
eler. My dear, I see I frighten you as much as the rat.

VASALISA. Everything and everyone frightens me. When I
marry Prince Mishka, I pray I will have a child who will
be without fear and will love me always.

BABA YAGA. Love you always? Is that what you think happens when you have a child?

VASALISA. I hope I've been a small comfort to you. I'm
sorry I'm not my twin.

BABA YAGA. True, she is amusing, open hearted, her eyes
sparkle with life, but there is something to be said for
a bleak sourpuss. You have seen the dark underbelly of
those who live happily among others. I'd say you were
the perfect companion for a miserable old witch.

VASALISA. Soon my twin will have accomplished her goal.
The Prince will be mine and I will be leaving. My happiness will be my revenge upon all my t-t-tormenters.

BABA YAGA. If you believe that, then you are a fool. You do
not love him. You wish to acquire him as a weapon.

VASALISA. I am not a fool. Please, do not call me that.

(The **BABA YAGA** *takes her cane and conjures up a pool
of water.)*

BABA YAGA. Look at your reflection in the pond. Tell me if
you do not see the greatest fool of all.

VASALISA. I do not wish to look.

BABA YAGA. Look in the water, child! You are afraid not to.
Go on. Go on!

(**VASALISA** *steps forward and looks into the pond. She is horrorstruck.*)

BABA YAGA. Tell me, girl, what do you see?

VASALISA. I see your face. No, No. You evil witch. It's not so. I am not you! I am not you! (**VASALISA** *runs off in tears.*)

Scene Fourteen

(The lab. ZYGOTE enters stealthily and goes to the desk. He takes a key out of his pocket and opens it, searching for drugs. CONSTANCE enters and catches him.)

CONSTANCE. Why bother breaking in? Don't I always give you the SP 596 that you crave?

ZYGOTE. I was looking for morphine. Spreading it around town makes me quite the popular fellow.

CONSTANCE. Did you make that key? You're very clever. Did you also make the key to break into my files?

ZYGOTE. I haven't gone near your files.

CONSTANCE. You can drop your mask with me. Where are they? What have you done with them?

ZYGOTE. With what? What are you talking about?

CONSTANCE. The files. My research. The formula for human duplication.

ZYGOTE. I didn't take them. I swear I didn't.

CONSTANCE. You disgust me.

ZYGOTE. Don't say that.

CONSTANCE. How I rue the day you were fertilized in that Petri dish.

ZYGOTE. No, please, don't.

CONSTANCE. I knew the experiment was a failure from the start. I should have immediately washed the dish out with lye.

ZYGOTE. So now all is revealed. Your venom . Your essential cruelty.

CONSTANCE. Yes, at last all is revealed. I chose to keep you alive. I fed you. I protected you.

ZYGOTE. As a laboratory animal. A guinea pig. A rodent.

CONSTANCE. Any animal would have been more of a comfort. You've been nothing but a source of misery. A bitter mistake.

ZYGOTE. I tell you I didn't steal your files. It's not what you think.

CONSTANCE. Did you destroy them? They're meaningless to anyone else.

ZYGOTE. I didn't!

CONSTANCE. Did you derive pleasure in ripping them apart? *(She grabs him by the lapels.)*

ZYGOTE. Let go of me!

(ZYGOTE pulls away from her tight grip and runs out, leaving her devastated.)

CONSTANCE. Give them back to me! Give them back! Can't you comprehend what my work means to me? It's all I have! Please, give it back!

Scene Fifteen

*(Omaha. The scene continues. **PEG** and **DREW** enter from the kitchen.)*

DREW. What about the scene where the son was dying?

PEG. Really and truly. I loved the whole play. But have you considered a switcheroo and having the mother be the one who's dying?

DREW. That changes the whole thing.

PEG. No, it doesn't. Would be heartbreaking. I'll tell you what, let me take a crack at it. I'll strengthen the mother. Give it some well needed laughs. Beef up the suspense. Half the writers at Metro had me rework their scripts. Why are you looking at me like that? This is, after all, a first draft.

DREW. Who said it was a first draft? Oh boy. I'm such an idiot. Oh, I fell right into your trap.

PEG. You ask for my help, then you fly off the handle when I give it.

DREW. I'm not flying off the handle. And I didn't ask for your help. If I recall correctly, you rifled through my drawer and read a play of mine without my consent.

PEG. That is called a mother's love. And something your play is vitally missing.

DREW. Gee, I wonder why.

PEG. I had my failings, but I was a damn good mother. Why must I justify my existence to you? It's like I'm auditioning. For the past three years since my accident, I've been up for the role of your mother. When do I get put under contract? Drew, I'm not getting any younger. I have so much to offer.

DREW. Mother,. I'll tell you why you're here. You're broke and washed up in the business. This producer at Republic, M. J. What's-his-name, has dangled a possibility –

PEG. More than a possibility.

DREW. A remote possibility in front of you like a carrot. You've never been able to discipline yourself to write a script without a contract. All this talk of my great genius. You think I'm a mediocre hack but you need me to make the deadline.

PEG. If that's the way you wanna look at it. I'm a big girl. I'll do fine without you. Always have. You had it easy, kid. Every door was opened to you.

DREW. That is absolutely not true. When I was starting out, you never called on any of your *deep friendships* in the industry to help me. You didn't want the competition.

PEG. I was your greatest champion. When I did introduce you to people, you were sullen and downright insulting. You should know, "the girls" have completely had it with your rudeness.

DREW. The girls? Their combined ages are older than the Magna Carta. One of the great pleasures of my Midwestern exile is not having to endure another dinner party of your coven; "the women who created Hollywood."

PEG. Thank God for Mary Pickford, Frances Marion, Anita Loos and Madeleine Andrews. Warm, loving women of achievement who go out of their way to help one another.

DREW. Madeleine Andrews? Warm? Loving? That cold fish?

PEG. Don't you dare criticize Maddy. She's a great friend and a top notch pro.

(Shift to Queenie's Penthouse. **ZYGOTE** *is preparing to give* **QUEENIE** *a morphine injection.* **PEG** *and* **DREW** *remain in Omaha as well.)*

QUEENIE. I wasn't Queenie Bartlett yet. Just a dame from Corkscrew Alley.

DREW. She bores me when I have to sit next to her and she's boring me now.

PEG. Well, right now I find you a crashing bore and I have no interest in speaking to you any further.

(She picks up a magazine. DREW sits and glares at her.)

ZYGOTE. The rumor mill has it that you had a steamy romance with Tyrone Power.

QUEENIE. I had one pleasant rendezvous with Mr. Power. He was always my favorite. *(He gives her the shot.)* Kid, you give a good injection. Didn't even feel a pinch. I sure can depend on you.

ZYGOTE. More than that ungrateful son of yours.

QUEENIE. Don't talk like that.

(DREW decides to break into Peg's silence.)

DREW. Mother, I can't go back to being your Frankenstein monster. Your worshipful drone. I can't go back to putting you to bed after you've drunk too much.

PEG. You never put me to bed in your life.

DREW. Oh, I frequently put you to bed!

PEG. I have had enough of being your punching bag. Really. That's it. That's it. I'm not going to take it anymore. Good luck to you, kid. I'll be on the next train out of here.

DREW. Let me find the schedule. Trains to Los Angeles don't run on the hour, you know.

PEG. To hell with the goddam schedule. If I have to, I'll wait at the goddam train station all goddam night. *(She exits.)*

ZYGOTE. I would never have treated you like he did.

QUEENIE. You're a good boy. I've gotta run.

ZYGOTE. Want me to go with you?

QUEENIE. No, no. You stay here and baby-sit the new addition. I won't be long.

(The doorbell rings. QUEENIE freezes.)

ZYGOTE. Expecting company?

QUEENIE. I bet it's a reporter wanting a quote about Senator Crenshaw's belly aching on organized crime.

ZYGOTE. I'll give him a quote in the solar plexus.

QUEENIE. Don't bother. I'll do a Houdini through the service elevator. See ya, kid. *(She exits.)*

(ZYGOTE answers the door. It's STEVE and VERNA.)

STEVE. You're here a lot, aren't you?

ZYGOTE. I make myself useful.

STEVE. Where's my mother?

ZYGOTE. She's out.

STEVE. Out where?

ZYGOTE. I'd rather not say.

STEVE. I wanna know what's going on with my mother.

ZYGOTE. If you loved her you wouldn't need me to answer your questions.

STEVE. Who the hell are you to tell me how much I love my mother?

ZYGOTE. I know how much you've hurt her. And you'll hurt her again by bringing this tramp around.

(STEVE grabs ZYGOTE by the collar.)

VERNA. Put the circus freak out of his misery.

ZYGOTE. I may be ugly but jealousy is making you positively green.

STEVE. Me? Jealous of you? Ha!

ZYGOTE. I've become your Mama's best buddy. We have lots of fun together. She's teaching me how to play Canasta. I'm the only one she can trust. She calls me her "keeper of the secrets."

STEVE. What secrets? What do you know?

VERNA. Don't listen to him, Steve. He's bluffin'.

ZYGOTE. Let's find some private little place to talk. Oh, I forget, you can't handle small places. Poor Stevie might wet himself.

STEVE. I swear I'm gonna kill you, Pinhead, but not today 'cause when I do I wanna take a nice long time with it. Now, get out!

ZYGOTE. May I get my things from the other room? I've been staying here, you know.

STEVE. Get your stuff and put your hat on. That toupee of yours reeks of something awful.

ZYGOTE. It's not the toupee. I expel gas through my ears. *(ZYGOTE exits into the bedroom.)*

STEVE. Just when I thought I'd heard everything.

VERNA. Did you see him wiggling them ears? I bet he was stinking up the joint on purpose.

(QUEENIE enters from the bedroom. It's not Queenie, but her clone, QUEENIE 2.)

STEVE. Ma, I thought you were out. Aw Ma, I can't tell you how much I've missed you. I'm miserable when we're not speaking.

QUEENIE 2. Are you my son? Do I love you? I do.

STEVE. I love you. *(They embrace.)* You look great, Ma. Been to one of them health farms in the desert?

VERNA. Mother Bartlett...

QUEENIE 2. Mother?

VERNA. I'm sorry that we've gotten off on the wrong foot.

QUEENIE 2. Who's this?

STEVE. You want to start all over again. Don't you? Aw, Ma, you're the best. What do you say I take both my girls out to lunch?

QUEENIE 2. Both? Only one of us is here.

VERNA. *(wary)* Steve, I'll wait for you outside in the Ford Vedette. *(She exits.)*

STEVE. Yeah, you're definitely yourself again. Ma, there's only one of you.

(QUEENIE 2 exits. PEG enters with a suitcase and wearing her overcoat. The actor playing STEVE returns to being DREW and lowers his head as if he's having trouble catching his breath.)

PEG. Drew, just remember, you have only one mother and you've chased her out the door in thirty degree weather.

DREW. I haven't chased you out the door. You're indomitable. You barge in. You take over.

PEG. *(notices his breathing)* What's wrong? Are you all right?

DREW. Yeah, I'm all right.

PEG. You're breathing funny.

DREW. My heart is pounding. I can't catch my breath.

PEG. Do you feel shooting pains in your arm?

DREW. I'm not sure. You think I'm having a heart attack?

PEG. Of course not. I'm not saying that. I was just asking.

DREW. I've never felt this way before.

PEG. I'm driving you to the hospital. I want you checked out. *(She grabs his jacket.)*

DREW. I'm fine. Really, I'm fine. *(He feels more pain.)* Oh Jesus.

PEG. *(terrified)* Oh, please, God. You're gonna be okay. This is just – Come on. Let's get in the car.

DREW. Don't be frightened, Mother. Oh God, my heart really feels like it's about to explode out of my chest. Hey, weren't you there when John Gilbert had his heart attack?

PEG. This is no time for stories. *(They exit out the front door.)*

End of Act One

ACT TWO

Scene One

(The fairy tale past. The **BABA YAGA** *and* **VASALISA TWO** *enter from the darkness of the hut. The double is carrying a beautiful woven shawl.)*

VASALISA TWO. Baba Yaga, you must see the shawl in the sunlight.

BABA YAGA. The sun is not my friend.

VASALISA TWO. But notice the many colors of the wool. How pretty it shall look upon your frail shoulders.

BABA YAGA. My sweet creation, how ever did you find time to complete such a masterpiece of knitting? You have been so busy seducing the Prince. I imagine by now he is very much in love with you. And perhaps you with him.

VASALISA TWO. It is Vasalisa he will love and I pray will marry very soon.

BABA YAGA. My dear, you can drop your mask with me.

VASALISA TWO. I wear no mask. Last evening, as Prince Mishka and I strolled under the cherry blossoms, he told me he loved me.

BABA YAGA. *(stunned)* I never thought it would happen so quickly.

VASALISA TWO. Is that not wonderful? I had Vasalisa run to the palace for I knew Prince Mishka would be there waiting for her. Indeed, when she arrived, he asked her to marry him and she has accepted.

BABA YAGA. Why was I not told of this? How dare you keep it a secret?

VASALISA TWO. But are you not pleased? This was the moment we have worked towards. Our every dream. Soon Vasalisa will leave this dark forest forever to be the beloved bride of Prince Mishka.

BABA YAGA. You fool, I am not ready for her to go.

VASALISA TWO. But Baba Yaga –

BABA YAGA. No, no, this cannot be.

VASALISA TWO. I only did your bidding.

BABA YAGA. How cruel to take my girl from me so soon. You hateful creature.

VASALISA TWO. Do not say that.

BABA YAGA. How I wish you had never been born. Go away! I can't bear the sight of you.

VASALISA TWO. Baba Yaga!

BABA YAGA. Go away!

(The **BABA YAGA,** *terribly distraught, goes inside her hut, leaving* **VASALISA TWO** *very confused.)*

Scene Two

(Omaha, the living room. Several hours later. **PEG** *and* **DREW** *enter through the front door, having just driven back from the hospital. They both look drained.* **DREW** *lies down on the sofa.)*

PEG. Darling, it was all in your head. All in your head. One of these days you really will work yourself up to a heart attack. I could kill you for putting us through this today. I'm so relieved there was nothing physically wrong with you.

DREW. Well, there wasn't when we left the hospital. The drive back may have permanently dislodged my vertebrae. There is a reason why you've been in six car accidents. You don't know how to drive.

PEG. Count it among my many failings.

DREW. I'll concede that you weren't any worse a parent than others of your ilk.

PEG. How generous of you.

DREW. I say that with great tenderness. None of you picture people should have had children. Writers, actors, directors, producers. Every kid I know turned out bad.

PEG. My dear, there are plenty of offspring of postal employees who today are lying on psychoanalysts' couches. Look at my parents. A salt of the earth pharmacist and his wife. They regularly beat me with a strap for the slightest infraction. There are things I've never told you about my childhood. Things I've never told anyone. I don't even discuss them with myself.

DREW. That sounds cryptic.

PEG. The last thing I mean to be is melodramatic. There are some memories, my boy, which you file away on an upper shelf. I've tried my best to shield you from my personal problems so you wouldn't grow up neurotic.

DREW. Mother, don't count that among your successes.

Scene Three

(Dr. Rutenspitz's apartment. **PEG** *has returned to being* **DR. RUTENSPITZ.** **CONSTANCE** *enters from another room. Her hair is loose about her shoulders.)*

DR. RUTENSPITZ. Were you able to close your eyes for a few minutes? A short nap will cure most ills. I wish I had more to offer. I don't know how it happened that I'm out of coffee. I'll fix you a drink. *(She crosses to the liquor cabinet.)*

CONSTANCE. Thank you but automatons do not consume alcohol. And as you know, I'm a robot with no human feelings. Well, perhaps we should experiment and see if gin warps the mechanism. Do you have the *formula* for a perfect martini?

DR. RUTENSPITZ. I'm pouring you a small glass of Schnapps.

CONSTANCE. Dr. R, didn't you notice my cunning use of the word "formula?" It's missing. All the research files empty. Years of work obliterated.

DR. RUTENSPITZ. I suspected as much. *(She hands* **CONSTANCE** *the drink.)*

CONSTANCE. Zygote should have been destroyed at his conception. I was warned by everyone. I was too arrogant to listen.

DR. RUTENSPITZ. Have you proof Zygote stole the files?

CONSTANCE. There's no one else. And it wasn't Queenie Bartlett. She doesn't have the knowledge or means to use the formula to create a human double. It had to be Zygote.

Dr. **RUTENSPITZ.** I imagine you have made some attempt to reconstruct the stolen materials?

CONSTANCE. It's hopeless. A great miserable failure. I could have almost predicted it.

DR. RUTENSPITZ. How so?

CONSTANCE. I try too hard. I'm humorless. Miracles don't happen to my kind.

DR. RUTENSPITZ. At this point, I'd recommend a change of direction. Perhaps working with children.

CONSTANCE. I have no interest in unformed brains, unless they're pickled in formaldehyde.

DR. RUTENSPITZ. It might prove therapeutic. You could tell them stories.

CONSTANCE. I don't know any stories. I've always been afraid of children. Years ago, I worked for a city health clinic in New York. Late one wintry afternoon, an old immigrant woman came in with a broken wrist, accompanied by her granddaughter. The girl was fifteen, though she appeared much younger. This child would have definitely intrigued you.

DR. RUTENSPITZ. Why is that?

CONSTANCE. She was delicate, not particularly pretty and excruciatingly shy. It took prodding for her to even reveal her name. Margaret. However, I sensed immediately that there was true intelligence hidden there. And this almost painful sensitivity. We barely exchanged a word and yet it was as if we were in perfect sympathy with each other. I thought, now this is someone I could help. Perhaps with her caring ways, she could grow up to be a nurse. Maybe even a doctor. And I would gain so much from knowing this child. The two of us. Margaret and me.

DR. RUTENSPITZ. You contacted the girls' family?

CONSTANCE. I wrote them; explaining that I believed their daughter to be exceptional and wished to take her under my wing. It was a frustrating few weeks before I received a letter from her mother. She was grateful for my proposal and arranged for me to meet Margaret the following Saturday at Columbus Circle, at the edge of the park. I was nervous at the prospect of seeing her again but Margaret surprised me by immediately kissing me on the cheek. A familiarity I found a tad excessive. I expressed that I would like very much to be her mentor. She thanked me profusely. She was remarkably outgoing and gregarious. So different from her reserved manner at the clinic. I apologize for the length of this anecdote. I'm not accustomed to telling stories.

DR. RUTENSPITZ. Do go on. My interest has been more than piqued.

CONSTANCE. Then I'll help myself to another Schnapps. It seems to make me more, um loquacious. For several months, Margaret came over at least four times a week. She was an excellent student and flourished under my guidance. She was always full of good humor and physically demonstrative. A hug around my waist, her head leaning against my shoulder.

DR. RUTENSPITZ. Like a daughter.

CONSTANCE. Something kept me from returning her affection. There was a quality missing that I never saw again after that first meeting at the clinic. The beautiful sadness. The poetic silence was gone. Late one afternoon, we were discussing a paper she had written on Dostoyevsky's novella *The Double.* The element of the book that seemed to haunt her was the tragedy of two people sharing one identity.

DR. RUTENSPITZ. How did you respond?

CONSTANCE. My response was that there were numerous and grave spelling errors and an appalling use of the subjunctive. Margaret burst into tears. I said, "My dear, whatever could be the matter?" She said she could no longer go on with this deceit. She was in fact not Margaret at all but Maureen.

DR. RUTENSPITZ. What?

CONSTANCE. She was Margaret's twin sister. Yes. There were two of them. It seems that Margaret didn't want to accept my offer. She told Maureen that I had frightened her at our first meeting in the clinic. I had misread her every look. She thought me cold and forbidding; a witch in a fairy tale. However, her high spirited sister found my proposal to be the answer to her dreams. It was Maureen who wrote me, at this point pretending to be her own mother.

DR. RUTENSPITZ. Weren't you touched by the girl's enthusiasm to learn?

CONSTANCE. I was furious that I'd been duped. Heartsick at being rejected by one so like me at her age. *(near tears)* If there was a genuine pair of twins, it was the real Margaret and me. Why wasn't she able to see that? I called the imposter a hateful, pathological liar. I told her she'd never amount to anything in life because she was morally bankrupt. She sobbed that she had done all she could to make me love her. I refused to listen. I grabbed her by the wrist, pushed her out the door and bolted it shut.

DR. RUTENSPITZ. Oh, my dear.

CONSTANCE. She banged her fists against the door, pleading for me to take her back. I've erased it from my mind for so long. I've always prided myself on my ability to put ugly truths behind me. Don't look back. Do your work. Full steam ahead. Oh God. Oh God, I don't want to be an automaton. I want to breathe. Where's my coat? Where did I put it? *(She rises.)*

DR. RUTENSPITZ. Where are you going?

CONSTANCE. There's someone I have to see. Someone who makes me feel just a little bit human. *(exits)*

Scene Four

(Omaha. The living room. The scene continues.)

PEG. Drew, you spend too much time in Hamlet-like soul searching in your writing and your life. For God's sake, dive into a pool of piranhas. Jump off the cliff. Leap over the volcano.

DREW. I suppose I get my introspective nature from my father.

PEG. You've got to be kidding. Your father has never had a deep thought in his life.

DREW. My father enjoys his work as a mailman because it gives him time to reflect on the world.

PEG. Did he tell you this?

DREW. He didn't have to. These past three months have been very special to Dad and me. We rarely need words. We can spend a beautiful day together almost without speaking. I've discovered that at heart I'm very much a Nebraskan the same as Dad and his father and his father before him. Unlike you, I can derive the greatest pleasure from simply looking at the colors of amber and purple that streak across the prairie skies. I've spent hours poring over Dad's family scrapbooks and I see myself. I look like my father's people. I am my father's son.

(beat)

PEG. I don't know how to tell you this. No, I won't. I can't do that. I should but I won't.

DREW. What are you mumbling about?

PEG. I could drop such a bombshell on you, but I swore I wouldn't and I won't.

DREW. What bombshell?

PEG. There is no bombshell.

DREW. Just spill it.

PEG. How I've dreaded this moment.

DREW. My father is not my father.

PEG. How did you know?

DREW. Because I know how you write. I know how you build a scene.

PEG. What have you to say about that?

DREW. You are the most amazing – no, that sounds like a compliment. It's so clear. You have to damage my relationship with Dad, so I'll return and write your screenplay with you.

PEG. The simple fact is he's not your father. Not by birth.

DREW. No, the simple fact is you find it impossible to accept that I might have any allegiance or even affection for anyone else. Any possibility of that is a betrayal of you. What then is the story? Who is my real father?

PEG. I couldn't say. Hollywood was a very different town in the teens. We worked all day and played all night.

DREW. And you were quite the popular gal.

PEG. I wasn't lonely. But I did find myself in a difficult position. As free-thinking as my circle was, I could not parade about a child born out of wedlock. My only recourse was to come home to Nebraska. One afternoon, a young postman came to deliver the mail and it turned out that we'd known each other in school. He was sympathetic to my plight and offered to marry me and give my unborn child his name. I made it clear that I had every intention of returning immediately to Los Angeles after my child's birth and filing for divorce. I thought he understood and was fine with it. However, after you were born, he became sentimental and grew to actually believe you were his flesh and blood.

DREW. What a despicable man.

PEG. I was certainly not going to become a postman's wife in Nebraska, so I was forced to escape in the dark of night with the wee babe in my arms.

(**DREW** *throws his head back in laughter.*)

PEG. Drew?

DREW. Mother, you slay me! You slay me!

PEG. Don't get yourself worked up.

DREW. It never occurred to you before to give me the low-down on my birth?

PEG. I suppose I should have told you years ago but I was afraid –

DREW. You'd lose me?

PEG. Drew, you must believe me that my love for you is the only pure, beautiful thing in my entire awful life.

    (**DREW** *exits into the kitchen and* **PEG** *follows him.*)

Scene Five

(A department store try-on room. **VERNA** *and Queenie's clone,* **QUEENIE 2,** *enter.* **VERNA** *carries a gold lame dress.)*

VERNA. We're lucky it's raining. This place is usually a mad-house. Awfully sweet of Steve to let us gals get in a little shopping. Bullocks has the swankiest dressing rooms in town.

QUEENIE 2. So many pretty things out there. I want them all.

VERNA. We shouldn't keep him waiting. You know how Steve is when he blows his topper.

QUEENIE 2. Verna, give me more of those um eat 'ems.

VERNA. Oh, the chocolate bonbons. Glad you liked 'em. But you finished the whole bag. And, after all those digs about my big can. *(She holds up a gold dress.)* Not sure how crazy I am for this dress. I don't like anything that masks my curves.

QUEENIE 2. Ooh. Gold. Shiny. Pretty.

VERNA. Well, bless my blonde heart, I wouldn't have thought that was quite your style. I always think of you as pure Chanel.

QUEENIE 2. Really? Is that what I am? Ooh, I want to buy everything. Hats. Shoes. Scarves. The works. And then I want Steve to take us dancing. He will, won't he? I want to dance my feet off. I want to dance till I drop. *(QUEENIE begins to rhumba.)*

VERNA. Sister, I certainly had you pegged wrong.

QUEENIE 2. You don't know me. Nobody knows me.

(Her dancing becomes more frenetic, till she gets dizzy and nearly topples over.)

VERNA. Lady, if I didn't know you better, I'd swear you were on a toot.

*(**VERNA** gets out of her dress and slips into the gold lame dress.)*

QUEENIE 2. I'd like to be on a toot, whatever that is. I wanna go to a movie. I want to see a movie with Tyrone Power. I love Tyrone Power.

VERNA. I've always had a bit of a yen for Ty Power myself. What did you think of "The Razor's Edge?" A little highbrow for my tastes.

QUEENIE 2. Didn't see that one.

VERNA. I bet you liked him in "Johnny Apollo."

QUEENIE 2. Don't know that one.

VERNA. I thought you said you loved Tyrone Power.

QUEENIE 2. I just love him. Stop asking me things. Try that dress on.

VERNA. I will.

*(***VERNA*** turns her back on ***QUEENIE 2***, while she slips the gold lame dress on over her head.)*

VERNA. Wasn't sure if I should step into this one or pull it over my head. Could you give me a hand?

*(While ***VERNA*** struggles with the dress, ***QUEENIE 2*** digs into her purse.)*

VERNA. I really need some help. Are you there, Mrs. B? Jeeze.

*(***VERNA*** finally manages to pull the dress down over her head and shoulders. She looks up and sees ***QUEENIE 2*** impassively pointing a gun at her.)*

VERNA. Mother Bartlett, what – what are you doing?

QUEENIE 2. I know who you are. I know what you're after.

VERNA. You're not well. You're not yourself.

QUEENIE 2. I am myself. And I'm wise to the whole picture. Queenie told me everything. And there are things she didn't have to tell me.

VERNA. But you are Queenie. Honey, why don't you sit down? I'll have them bring you some water.

QUEENIE 2. Don't move. It'll be better for you if I shoot you once cleanly between the eyes.

VERNA. She did it, didn't she? You're not Queenie. You're the other one. The double. You've just been born, haven't you?

QUEENIE 2. I must do this for Steve. He is everything.

VERNA. He's everything to me too. Whoever you are, I love him.

QUEENIE 2. You're the enemy. Queenie told me. "The double crossing, two-faced whore is Crenshaw's girl. Since day one she's been on the government payroll. She's out to destroy our boy."

VERNA. Yes, I was for hire, but once I was in, I honestly fell in love with Steve.

QUEENIE 2. You want to hurt my baby. You wanna cut him up.

VERNA. What are you saying? No. No. It's not that way at all. I've been acting as a double agent but I've never given them one shred of information that'll do them any good.

QUEENIE 2. You're a liar! *(QUEENIE raises the gun to fire.)*

VERNA. Queenie doesn't want you to do this. She might have thought it, but she'd never pull the trigger. You're taking your cue from her private thoughts. Aren't you? But that's not fair. We think lots of awful things that we don't really want done. She didn't really ask you to kill Verna. Admit it. She didn't. Did she?

QUEENIE 2. She doesn't have to ask me. I just know she wants it. If she wants it, I want it. It's done.

(QUEENIE 2 calmly shoots VERNA dead. She picks up the dress.)

QUEENIE 2. I wonder if they have this in a smaller size.

Scene Six

(Queenie's penthouse. **STEVE** *enters and confronts his mother. She puts her bag on the desk.)*

QUEENIE. What are you? Insane? Of course I wouldn't kill Verna. Yes, I didn't like her. Yes, I knew she was out to betray us both. Yes, she dressed like a carnival cootch dancer. But no, I didn't kill her or order her to be killed.

STEVE. Ma, don't lie to me. People saw you.

QUEENIE. Who are these witnesses? Give me their names. Your girl was singing to the feds. Maybe they ordered the hit. They do that to their own.

STEVE. Don't lie to me. You've never lied to me.

QUEENIE. Then why would I start now? Son, I'm not sorry to see that creature dead.

STEVE. Ma.

QUEENIE. She was bad. I knew it from the beginning.

STEVE. Stop it.

QUEENIE. I have people high up who told me the wolf was in the sheepfold. My mistake was not warning you. I knew you loved her. If I told you she was working for the other side, I was afraid I'd lose you. My love for you is the only pure, beautiful thing in my entire awful life.

Scene Seven

(The lobby of Los Angeles' Philharmonic Hall. It's inter-mission and **ZYGOTE** *and* **QUEENIE 2** *are mingling in the crowd.* **ZYGOTE***, fragile in a tuxedo, reads aloud from his program.)*

ZYGOTE. Queenie, I think you'll find this of interest. "The Los Angeles Philharmonic owes its birth to William Andrews Clark, Jr., a multi-millionaire and amateur musician, who established Los Angeles first perma-nent symphony orchestra in 1919."

QUEENIE 2. How long will it be before the music starts up again?

ZYGOTE. Intermission usually lasts about fifteen minutes. You liked the Tchaikovsky?

QUEENIE 2. Crazy about it. I love music. So does Queenie. My first fella played the harmonica after we made love in the alley behind the wax museum. Should I think that's bad? I dunno. Did you ever make love in an alley?

ZYGOTE. *(embarrassed)* Queenie, people don't ask such things. This part is interesting. "Following its opening season, the orchestra made Philharmonic Auditorium on the North East corner of Fifth and Olive Streets its home."

QUEENIE 2. You're feeling sick, aren't you? That scares you.

ZYGOTE. I'm feeling fine. This program is filled with inter-esting facts.

QUEENIE 2. That lady in the red Balenciaga is staring at you. She's making a face to her friend.

ZYGOTE. Doesn't matter. Happens all the time.

QUEENIE 2. Lady, what are you lookin' at? Seen your own ugly mug in the mirror? I'd like to claw her face off. *(suddenly turns sweet again)* Why does everyone stare at you? I think you're cute. I once went to bed with a deaf piano salesman in Cleveland. Golly, I think I know what a piano is but what the hell's a Cleveland? Is he here? Have you seen him?

ZYGOTE. Who? The piano salesman?

QUEENIE 2. No, silly. Senator Crenshaw. He's supposed to be here tonight.

ZYGOTE. Is that why you wanted to come to the concert?

QUEENIE 2. He's so mean to Queenie and Steve. He wants to hurt them bad. Why?

ZYGOTE. *(suspecting she's packing a rod)* What's in your bag? A sack full of those chocolate bon bons you like so much? Would you give me one?

QUEENIE 2. Never ask a lady what she keeps in her bag. Poor baby had no Mama to teach him manners. Read me some more about the orchestra. Go on. Please.

ZYGOTE. "The current music director is Alfred Wallenstein. He is the fifth to be appointed to this post since Walter Henry Rothwell conducted the Orchestra's premiere performance in 1919.

*(**ZYGOTE** looks up and sees that **QUEENIE 2** has disappeared. He becomes alarmed.)*

ZYGOTE. Queenie? Queenie? Queenie?

*(**ZYGOTE** runs off.)*

Scene Eight

(The Lab. STEVE *visits* CONSTANCE.*)*

CONSTANCE. Thank you for coming here. I would have met you anywhere you wanted.

STEVE. Under the circumstances, it was safer for me to come to you.

CONSTANCE. How can you be so sure your mother killed Verna?

STEVE. She was seen by ten - twenty witnesses going into that fitting room. Ma came out of the store alone. Made up some cock-and-bull story that Verna wanted to do more shopping and would catch up with us later. Ma always hated Verna.

CONSTANCE. But enough to kill her?

STEVE. She says she has proof that Verna was working for the feds. That everything between us from the very beginning was a lie.

CONSTANCE. Do you believe her?

STEVE. Yeah, I believe her. I'm sweating. You really need some fresh air in here.

CONSTANCE. Where's your mother now?

STEVE. Don't you read the papers or listen to the radio?

CONSTANCE. I try not to.

STEVE. Ma's the biggest news in the world right now. She killed a United States senator.

CONSTANCE. Stephen, what are you saying?

STEVE. She bumped off Senator Crenshaw. She shot him while he was at a concert at Philharmonic Auditorium. She's out for revenge on anyone who's done us dirt. That's what makes no sense. In her entire career, she's almost never had to play rough. That's her genius. Why should she suddenly go crazy and start rubbing people out?

CONSTANCE. Your mother's not well. I mean that physically. She's very ill. She's been taking many strong medications. That can certainly cloud judgment.

STEVE. I'm not feeling very good. Have I got a temperature?

CONSTANCE. *(feels his forehead)* You may be slightly elevated.

STEVE. I can't take being in tight places. My Achilles heel, Ma calls it. We have a hideout in the Nevada desert. I'm certain that's where she's holing up. It's only a matter of time before the feds nab her. They'll take her dead or alive. I've got the shakes. I can't even stand up.

CONSTANCE. Yes, you can. Claustrophobia is not a physical condition.

STEVE. Then why do I wanna die? *(He screams in agony.)* Oh God, Connie.

CONSTANCE. Darling, look into my eyes. Take a deep breath and begin counting backwards from fifty.

STEVE. What are you trying to do?

CONSTANCE. I'm going to hypnotize you. Concentrate on my eyes.

STEVE. That's not hard. I know we never could have made it. But I'll confess there have been times I've dreamed about us being together.

CONSTANCE. Perhaps we could. That's why I needed to see you.

STEVE. What are you saying?

CONSTANCE. I've lost everything I thought was important. I want to be a new Constance Hudson. The other one, the one with no feelings, is prepared to die. This one is ready to live.

STEVE. Now *you're* going crazy. I wouldn't let you do it.

CONSTANCE. Isn't that up to me to decide?

STEVE. Dr. Constance Hudson a gun moll? It ain't gonna happen.

CONSTANCE. Please, Steve. Take me with you. I'm not too proud to beg.

STEVE. I tell ya, I wouldn't let it happen. You've got important work to do. You've got a future.

CONSTANCE. Please, Steve, I can't go on the way I am.

STEVE. No, baby. And that's the end of that discussion. How am I gonna walk out of here?

(**ZYGOTE** *enters, looking very ill and fragile.*)

ZYGOTE. Dr. Hudson?

CONSTANCE. Zygote, you're ill.

ZYGOTE. Yes, Dr. Hudson. It seems I've reached my expiration date. It looks like public enemy number two isn't faring very well either.

STEVE. I'm gonna survive long enough to see you stuffed and mounted in a glass case. (**STEVE** *struggles to get up.*)

CONSTANCE. Stephen, be careful.

STEVE. Connie, thanks for those earlier sweet thoughts, but I'm gonna pretend you never said any of 'em. Never heard a word.

(**STEVE** *staggers out of the lab.*)

ZYGOTE. These are bad days for the Bartlett family.

CONSTANCE. How do you know them? How do you know Steve?

ZYGOTE. I'm a, shall we say, business connection to Mrs. Bartlett.

CONSTANCE. You sold her narcotics.

ZYGOTE. The feds are gonna kill her. To Queenie it would be a kind of blessing. She just doesn't want to make it easy for them. You gotta love a dame like that.

(**ZYGOTE** *begins to gag and lose his balance.*)

CONSTANCE. Sit down.

ZYGOTE. Is my decline according to your statistics? Parts of my body have begun to turn lovely shades of amber and puce. I daren't take off my toupee. I have a terrible case of the runs.

CONSTANCE. All this would conform to my calculations.

ZYGOTE. Termination of the organism is near?

CONSTANCE. Very near, I'm afraid.

ZYGOTE. What perfect symmetry that I should end my life once more under your observation.

CONSTANCE. Do you think Mrs. Bartlett's recent violent behavior could be due to an interaction between her prescribed medications and the drugs you've sold her?

ZYGOTE. You don't know? You really don't know.

CONSTANCE. I can't know anything without full disclosure of the drugs in her body.

ZYGOTE. What a laugh. The brilliant Dr. Hudson is as ignorant as a child. Queenie Bartlett hasn't killed anyone. Well, not since she iced Jimmy the Nose in a phone booth twenty years ago.

(*ZYGOTE* *has a sudden intense rush of pain. He doubles over.* *CONSTANCE* *catches him.*)

CONSTANCE. Try to be still.

ZYGOTE. Dr. Hudson, at this moment you seem, dare I say, almost motherly. The pain is subsiding.

CONSTANCE. Once I came close to experiencing the fabled maternal instinct.

ZYGOTE. Were you "with child?"

CONSTANCE. I used my own eggs in an experiment.

ZYGOTE. My experiment?

(*CONSTANCE* *nods.*)

ZYGOTE. In some quarters, you could be considered my mother.

CONSTANCE. When I peered at the newly fertilized egg through the microscope, I felt a kind of love. It frightened me as I'd never been frightened before. But, you see, I could allow nothing to interfere with my objective study of your physical, neurological and emotional development.

ZYGOTE. Funny enough, I can almost fleeben porpif voo –

CONSTANCE. Zygote?

ZYGOTE. Pleeben bor – almost forgive you cor bat. But can you kurgrive – the person who bole – who stole fru gl-your – zee ul – fooral mala?

CONSTANCE. My formula? My cellular duplication formula?

(ZYGOTE nods.)

CONSTANCE. I know why you stole it. You felt neglected. You had a need to destroy me. You gave it to Mrs. Bartlett, didn't you? She's now in possession of it. That was your revenge.

ZYGOTE. It's mot zat. Oh, what does it matter? You have to see the – vubble poo cade –

CONSTANCE. See what?

ZYGOTE. Que—Quee – QUEENIE 2.

CONSTANCE. Where is she? Where is Queenie?

ZYGOTE. Pevad – P—p- qua—Nevada. Chuckawalala –

CONSTANCE. Chuckawalla, Nevada?

ZYGOTE. Rumeniss – pits.

CONSTANCE. Dr. Rutenspitz? What about Dr. Rutenspitz? I haven't been able to reach her for days. I've been terribly worried.

ZYGOTE. Buggamalla – walla.

CONSTANCE. What?

ZYGOTE. Coogagalla.

CONSTANCE. Chuckawalla? She's in Nevada with Queenie?

(ZYGOTE barely nods. He's fading fast.)

Queenie is holding her ransom, isn't she? She's using Dr. Rutenspitz as a human shield to protect herself from the FBI. That's correct, isn't it? Isn't it? Isn't it?

(ZYGOTE's hand falls limp. He's dead. The original experiment is over.)

Scene Nine

(Omaha. **PEG** *looks up from her notes.)*

PEG. Was that the wind blowing the shutters? What a lonely sound. You really like living by yourself?

DREW. Yep.

PEG. I hate it. The worst thing is not being able to laugh at catastrophes. When you were with me, if the car broke down or the stove caught fire, we'd turn it into a zany caper. Alone, it's just terrifying and sad.

DREW. You seem to go out a lot.

PEG. I try. I put on my brightest lipstick and a saucy hat and show up at parties but people look at me like I'm a ghost from the crazy old days.

DREW. What about the coven?

PEG. Mary never leaves her room at Pickfair. Lillian and Anita moved to New York. Madeleine has her young protégés. Frances is obsessed with her sculpture and Adela has turned to Jesus. I could use a hobby. Maybe I should get hooked on pills.

DREW. We're really dipping into the cauldron of self pity. Aren't we?

PEG. With both hands, baby. I'm back to being the same lonely oddball kid I was in Nebraska. Yucch.

DREW. You're the shy Princess Vasalisa in that fairy tale I loved so much. And you transformed yourself into your own fabulous twin.

PEG. I feel more like the old witch.

DREW. It's a good story. I suppose that's why it's lasted hundreds of years.

PEG. Oh honey, that's not an authentic Russian fairy tale. I made up that story to comfort you, because you felt like such a misfit.

DREW. You made it up?

PEG. I cobbled together several stories and added my own twist. I'm a storyteller. That's what I do. And now I've lost the touch.

DREW. You'll find a writing assignment.

PEG. You're missing the point. I can't write anymore. I can't believe I'm saying this. I have no shortage of ideas. I come up with a different one every day. But when I sit down at the typewriter or even put pen to paper, nothing happens. I'm so frightened.

(PEG begins to sob. DREW gently holds her.)

DREW. Every writer goes through something like this. It passes.

PEG. Living alone has aged me. It's dulling my edge. I'm so scared, Drew. I'm so scared.

DREW. You're as sharp as a steak knife at Mussos.

PEG. Kid, you gotta help me.

DREW. I can't – I can't write this script for you.

PEG. We'll inspire each other. You'll spark me. We're good for each other.

DREW. I can't go back with you. I just can't.

PEG. Please.

DREW. I can't.

PEG. *(PEG pulls herself together)* Oh my. I've really made a mess of myself. Gotta think up. Up! Up! Up! That's the ticket. Energy stimulates the imagination and the imagination creates opportunity. That's the Aries in me coming out. I keep seeing a lonely, battered old house in the middle of the desert. Somehow the Queen of the mob and her son end up there and have to patch things up.

DREW. Mother, stop.

PEG. Early evening. A hideout. Worn shutters smacking against the house. Sagebrush blowing in the wind. The mob queen sits by the campfire shivering in a fabulous mink coat.

(QUEENIE enters in a mink coat.)

The gangster son joins her.

(DREW turns up his jacket collar as he becomes STEVE.)

He has his collar turned up. They always have their collars turned up.

Scene Ten

(Chuckawalla, Nevada. Midnight. **QUEENIE** *and*
STEVE *warm their hands by the campfire.)*

QUEENIE. Steve, don't blame yourself. It makes perfect
sense that you'd think I killed Verna. How could you
have known that I had a double who could read my
mind and was knocking off my enemies. Lord knows
it's not your everyday situation.

STEVE. I should have guessed it. After all, you did have
Connie on the payroll to create such a thing.

QUEENIE. Shhhh. Queenie's sleeping. And for God's sake,
don't call her a "thing." She's very touchy.

STEVE. What are we going to do with her? Frankly, she gives
me the willies.

QUEENIE. When she's not a merciless killing machine, she's
really rather dear. She's um – what's the word I'm
thinking of? She's guileless.

STEVE. Ma, there's no one like you.

QUEENIE. Under the circumstances, that statement doesn't
quite hold up.

STEVE. We can't let her go on murdering any sucker who
looks at us the wrong way. Your reputation is suffering,
Ma.

QUEENIE. I know. She's gotta go. But it's gonna be like killing a part of myself.

STEVE. Did you honestly think that I wouldn't eventually
have figured out she was an impostor? You and I are
the real twins. I'm the one who does your every bidding and I'm happy to do it.

QUEENIE. Baby, I don't know what I was thinking. All I
knew was that I had to protect you. I can't leave you in
an ugly world with no one on your side.

STEVE. How much time do the doctors give you?

QUEENIE. Hard to predict. Despite all their heroic efforts,
this thing inside me keeps growing. Kid, at a certain
point, I may have to ask you to help me pull off the
dutch act.

STEVE. Help you knock yourself off? Don't ask me to do that.

QUEENIE. I may not be able to ask you. You'll just have to know when the time is right. I'll be counting on that. And when the moment comes, I want you to think of it as a beautiful gift. That'll make it easier for you. So we're square?

STEVE. We're square.

QUEENIE. Hey, what's that?

STEVE. Probably another coyote.

QUEENIE. Personally, I'd give the desert back to the Indians. Say, that's no coyote. Get in the house.

(She pulls out her gun.)

STEVE. Ma, let me take care of this.

QUEENIE. Get in the house, I say.

STEVE. I've got you covered.

(Apprehensively, **STEVE** *goes inside.)*

QUEENIE. Whoever's out there, be a man and show your face.

(CONSTANCE, *wearing a trench coat and hat, enters also carrying a gun.)*

CONSTANCE. Mrs. Bartlett, it is I, Dr. Constance Hudson.

QUEENIE. Go back to your Bunsen burner, Dr. Hudson. I'm warning you.

CONSTANCE. I'm not afraid of you, Mrs. Bartlett.

(QUEENIE *fires a warning shot.* **CONNIE** *nimbly ducks away.)*

QUEENIE. That was to show I mean business.

CONSTANCE. As a scientist with the manual dexterity to pluck the nucleus from an embryo, I'm quite confident of the accuracy of my aim.

*(***CONSTANCE*** fires a shot, narrowly missing ***QUEENIE***.)*

QUEENIE. Not bad, honey. Not bad. But Dr. Hudson, don't forget I'm the one in the catbird seat. I'm the gal who knows her days are numbered.

CONSTANCE. You're not going to kill me, Mrs. Bartlett.

QUEENIE. If you come one step nearer I will. I've gotten everything I want out of you.

CONSTANCE. There's only one thing I want from you and when I get it, I shall gladly leave Chuckawalla.

QUEENIE. And what's that?

CONSTANCE. I know you're holding my colleague, Dr. Rutenspitz, hostage. I want you to let her go.

QUEENIE. All you had to do was ask. There was no need to fire guns and make vulgar threats. *(calling inside)* Hilda! You have a visitor!

CONSTANCE. There shall be a stiff penalty if you've harmed a hair on her head.

*(**DR. RUTENSPITZ** comes out of the house. **CONSTANCE** rushes toward her.)*

DR. RUTENSPITZ. My dear Connie, you are the last person I imagined out here in the desert.

CONSTANCE. Are you all right? I've been so worried.

QUEENIE. I'm going inside to make a fresh pot of coffee. Hilda, you want a cup?

DR. RUTENSPITZ. No, thank you, dear. Connie, how did you know I was here?

*(**QUEENIE** goes into the house.)*

CONSTANCE. Zygote told me. When did they abduct you?

DR. RUTENSPITZ. What exactly did Zygote say?

CONSTANCE. Not very much, I'm afraid. He was dying. And in his last moments, rapidly lost the power of speech. I was able to deduce that you were being held hostage by the Bartletts.

DR. RUTENSPITZ. Connie, I am not, nor have I ever been in any danger, at least, not from the Bartletts. Queenie, in fact, brought with her the finest liverwurst and sauerkraut I have ever tasted.

CONSTANCE. Have your new-found friends told you that they stole the formula? Or rather Zygote stole it for them.

DR. RUTENSPITZ. Connie, it was I who removed the data from the laboratory and sold the formula to Mrs. Bartlett, and for a very tidy sum.

CONSTANCE. You? You betrayed our great work? I don't believe it.

DR. RUTENSPITZ. I was so close to uncovering the secrets of molecular duplication. You, a much younger woman, exceedingly bright but not a true genius as I was, rode on my scientific coat tails. I tried very hard to fight my baser instincts of jealousy but in the end they won out. I had the courage that you lacked to proceed immediately with human experimentation. She's inside that house, you know.

CONSTANCE. She?

DR. RUTENSPITZ. The double. For lack of a better name, we call her QUEENIE 2.

CONSTANCE. That's what Zygote was trying to tell me.

DR. RUTENSPITZ. I think it's time you met your creation. *(calling inside the house)* Would you please send QUEENIE 2 out here? *(to CONSTANCE)* There have been some behavioral problems. QUEENIE 2 has all of Queenie One's deepest feelings but none of her life experience to handle them. Or rather she has the memory of the experience but learned nothing from it.

CONSTANCE. It was QUEENIE 2 who murdered Verna and Senator Crenshaw.

DR. RUTENSPITZ. She executed them, acting on Queenie One's unspoken desires.

(QUEENIE 2 enters from the house. CONSTANCE looks upon her in awe.)

QUEENIE 2. Queenie's teaching me to play poker but I always know when she's bluffing.

DR. RUTENSPITZ. My dear, this is a protégée of mine, Dr. Hudson.

QUEENIE 2. Protegee? Is that sort of like being your child?

DR. RUTENSPITZ. Not quite.

(**CONSTANCE** *goes over to the double and gently inspects the double's hands.*)

CONSTANCE. Extraordinary.

DR. RUTENSPITZ. Dr. Hudson has waited a very long time to meet you.

QUEENIE 2. Are you my sister?

CONSTANCE. No.

QUEENIE 2. My youngest brother, Herman, is a parish priest at St. Veronica's, 342 Otway. Crazy about Dachshunds. A limousine ran over a collie. We carried it to the side of the road.

CONSTANCE. I'm so sorry.

QUEENIE 2. Herman looks exactly like Uncle Ed. I mean, exactly. Uncle Ed was married eight times. He wanted to take us in but he couldn't. We had to stay in the orphanage. A woman there once told me a story about a princess who had a twin and a golden bird. A firebird. At the end, she flew away to the other side of the moon. *(sings)* "Shine on, Shine on harvest moon up in the sky." Aunt Mary Murgatroyd started out as a singer. She wore a wig ever since her hair fell out from a bad dye job. Sam Abatelli had to die. He didn't do the job. Taught me everything I needed to know about the numbers racket. My lucky number is seventy-two. 72 West Twenty-Third. Lonnie was only twenty-four when they got him. Bobby was hit twenty-five times. Why didn't they stop? Only twenty-six miles to the bridge. 27 Barrow Street. That's where they kept Stevie all tied up. He was only four years old. I had to kill six people to get the baby out of there alive. I got hit in the shoulder. Didn't I?

CONSTANCE. Don't try to remember everything. None of us can.

(**STEVE** *enters from the house.*)

STEVE. So Connie, what do you think of our new addition? I guess we're all expendable.

CONSTANCE. How long have you known?

STEVE. Don't be mad at me. I only found out when I got here.

QUEENIE 2. What are you two talking about? I don't like secrets.

CONSTANCE. There are so many things I want to ask you.

QUEENIE 2. I don't seem to have many answers.

CONSTANCE. How do you feel? Your tummy?

QUEENIE 2. I'm always hungry. Queenie loves steak, red and bloody. So do I.

CONSTANCE. Your head? Does it sometimes ache?

QUEENIE 2. No. Should it?

CONSTANCE. No. What's it like seeing everything for the first time?

QUEENIE 2. You ask a lot of questions.

CONSTANCE. I'm just so – so terribly pleased to meet you.

QUEENIE 2. You're soft and pretty. A princess in a fairy tale. Do you know any fairy tales?

CONSTANCE. No, but I'll make one up, if you'd like. I'll take QUEENIE 2 inside. She shouldn't get cold.

QUEENIE 2. Let's check in on Queenie. She wants a drink. She loves her bourbon, but she doesn't want to get tight. Do I like bourbon?

(**CONSTANCE** *gently takes* **QUEENIE 2** *inside the house.*)

STEVE. Lady, I gotta tell you, this little formula has created quite a set of problems. You know that nothing good can come of this.

DR. RUTENSPITZ. One can't place limits on the curiosity of man. He must go ever forward until his dreams inevitably destroy the planet.

STEVE. I'm not one to cast stones but stealing that formula away from Connie was pretty low. I thought you considered her like your own child. Not a very motherly thing to do.

DR. RUTENSPITZ. Connie is both a beloved daughter and a

bitter rival. I love her deeply yet need her to fail. Perhaps that is true of many parents and their offspring.

STEVE. Don't look here, Doc. My mother and I are the world to each other. The ground, the sky and everything in between.

(A great noise is heard overhead. The wind gathers force. It's an FBI helicopter.)

STEVE. They're here!

DR. RUTENSPITZ. Who? What is this? It's coming closer!

STEVE. The FBI!

(Suddenly there's wild gunfire from the helicopter.)

STEVE. Get down!

*(**STEVE** and **DR. R** are shot many times. We are back in Omaha. **PEG** drops Dr. R's glasses and lies on the floor. She sits up and is no longer the dead **DR. RUTENSPITZ**. **DREW** removes fedora and is lying on the rug, no longer the dead **STEVE**. **PEG** takes hold of **DREW** in her arms, improvising the story as Chuckawalla fades away. **DREW** tries to get away from her.)*

PEG. The FBI riddles the son with bullets. My gut feeling is the mother shouldn't be rubbed out. Not yet. She cradles the son in her arms. An underworld Pieta. Are you with me? We've got to write this down!

DREW. Mother, please. Let go of me.

PEG. All I'm saying is that at this point in the story…

DREW. Mother, I've got a story for you. A scorcher.

PEG. Wonderful. Shoot.

DREW. Three years ago when I got that phone call that you'd been in the car accident, I drove to the hospital and found you in that horrible trauma room. There was still blood in your hair. They told me you were going to die and this wave of intense panic swept over me. What would happen to me if you were gone? How could I exist in a world without you? Well, I had to be admitted to the hospital too. The psychiatric wing.

PEG. Drew, you're scaring me.

DREW. After I left you, I started going buggy, and was wandering around downtown muttering to myself in a way that was making a lot of people extremely nervous. I don't remember any of this, but evidently, I walked into a department store and ended up in the ladies try-on room. I guess I reverted back to when I was a little kid and you took me in there with you to get my opinion. The police came and carted me off to the mental ward.

PEG. How long did this go on?

DREW. Friday through Tuesday. And then it just went away. By the time you came out of the coma, I was strong enough to take care of you.

PEG. That's the wildest story I've ever heard.

DREW. I know I've been awful to you. I gripe and moan and accuse you of every crime against humanity. And what's the point? Some sort of half-hearted stab at independence? I moved all the way to Nebraska to get away from you. Well, I give up. You're the most fascinating person I'll ever know. I should just accept my fate and enjoy it. I'll go back to Los Angeles with you.

PEG. You can stop acting now. I get the satiric point.

DREW. I'm completely on the level. We always have fun together. I don't know why I'm forever trying to fight it. And I'll work on this outline with you. I can see the whole thing. Truly. The zombie, the lady scientist ... the mob queen. And she won't be a grotesque harridan like the mother in my play. The mob queen will have all sorts of colors and shadings. The mother in our movie will be a portrait you can be proud of. Let's keep going. Where were we? *(He gets back on the floor.)* The Mob Queen cradles the son in her arms? "An underworld Pieta," right?

*(Chuckawalla returns. **QUEENIE** comes out of the desert cabin. **PEG**, stunned by what he's just told her, returns to her chair. We're fully back in Chuckawalla now.)*

QUEENIE. Stephen! Stephen! Gotta get you out of here. They'll be back. Gotta get you to a doctor.

STEVE. No, Ma. If you get me to a hospital and I survive, the feds will put me away for good. Don't let them shut me away in some small dark place. I'd go permanently buggy.

QUEENIE. Hush, child.

STEVE. It hurts so bad. You gotta let me go, Ma. Help me.

QUEENIE. Don't ask me to do that. Please.

STEVE. We're running out of time. Ma, they'll never let me see you again. I couldn't bear it. To know you're out there and not be able to see you? Don't let 'em take me away, Ma. Please, don't let 'em take me. Remember what you said. It's a gift.

(**QUEENIE** *takes out her gun and fires it close to his skull. She cradles his body in her arms.*

QUEENIE. *(singing softly)* Shine on. Shine on, Harvest Moon, up in the sky ...

(Suddenly, another gunshot goes off from inside the desert cabin. Soon after, **CONSTANCE** *exits the house carrying her gun.)*

CONSTANCE. It was like killing a child. She told me her father took her to the end of the trolley line to gather wild flowers.

QUEENIE. That was *my* father.

CONSTANCE. *(She sees Stephen is dead.)* Stephen? Not Stephen.

(The loud sound and wind from the helicopter return again. **QUEENIE** *takes her gun and begins firing at it. An FBI agent shouts at them from his megaphone.)*

FBI AGENT *(V.O.)* Queenie Bartlett. We're prepared to kill all of you. Bartlett, give yourself up.

CONSTANCE. If they killed you, they'd be doing you a favor.

FBI AGENT *(V.O.)* Bartlett, we're giving you to the count of five to throw down your weapon. Then we shoot to kill. One!

CONSTANCE. Let's make a run for it. We can go up that path into the mountains.

FBI AGENT *(V.O.)* Two!

CONSTANCE. They'll never find us.

FBI AGENT *(V.O.)* Three!

QUEENIE. But Stephen?

CONSTANCE. He'd want you to save yourself. Let's go.

(**CONSTANCE** *grabs Queenie's arm and they run out.*)

(*We are now back in Omaha.* **DREW** *gets up off the floor.* **PEG** *is still reeling from Drew's confession. She knows in her heart what she must do. She has to push him out the door.*)

DREW. This is fantastic! Off they go into the mountains. Now let's start at the top. The mob queen wants the lady scientist to make her a double to protect her crazy son after her death.

PEG. Drew.

DREW. Yeah?

PEG. It's a pity you've never hit it off with Madeleine Andrews.

DREW. That's certainly the non sequitur of all time.

PEG. I know she comes off rather icy and forbidding, but in her youth Maddy was really quite a fun gal.

DREW. Okay.

PEG. Maddy found herself pregnant. A predicament for any girl, but truly would have signaled the absolute end to her budding career. All of us gals got together and pondered the situation carefully. How do we save Madeleine? I think it was Frances Marion who suggested that one of us secretly adopt the child. It certainly couldn't have been Lillian Gish or Mary Pickford, but I was in a position where I could go off with Madeleine to Omaha for a few months and then return to Los Angeles, the proud mother of a newborn.

DREW. Now you're telling me that you're not my mother? You do realize this is the third version I've heard of my birth.

PEG. I told you the third story is often the best. The first is the genesis of an idea, but usually completely off the track. The second is when you go overboard with flights of imagination. The third story is when you return to the truth. And this is the truth.

DREW. I don't know why you chose to tell me this now. Are you trying to punish me? I said I'd stay with you. You got what you wanted. Are you trying to get back at me for "abandoning" you for Dad? I've always known there was an ugly, vindictive side to you but it was never before focused on me. And it won't ever be again. You're going back to Los Angeles alone.

PEG. Are you staying here?

DREW. I don't know where I'll go. But it will be far away from you.

(He exits to the kitchen. **PEG** *sits on the sofa, emotionally spent.)*

(The Fairy Tale Past)

*(***VASALISA** *and* **BABA YAGA** *enter.)*

VASALISA. Baba Yaga, I-I-I see the truth. I hi-hid in the shadows of the palace and spied on Prince Mishka and my twin. He loves her, not me. And she loves and understands him, in ways I never could. She is now prepared to die so that I may become his bride.

BABA YAGA. Only one can wear his ring. One must vanish.

VASALISA. Baba Yaga, the double must remain in the role of Vasalisa and b-b-be the wife of the Prince. With all my heart, I wish them happiness. I will stay here in the forest. I know how t-t-terribly lonely you are and I promise to never leave you. I shall cook and clean and devote my life to your every need.

BABA YAGA. You would do that? You would remain here for the rest of my days?

VASALISA. Yes, I would.

BABA YAGA. Then you cannot stay.

VASALISA. Oh, please. Do not abandon me.

BABA YAGA. You cannot stay here for it is not good enough for you. Child, how I shall miss you but I cannot be guilty of such utter selfishness. *(She hears a faraway sound.)* Listen. Listen. What do you hear?

VASALISA. A large, powerful bird is flying toward us; its feathers bright as flame.

BABA YAGA. The firebird. She's come for you. You caught the feather. That was a sign. But you had to prove yourself worthy. And you have. The firebird rewards the pure of heart. Yes, my dear, you will climb upon her strong back and she will deliver you to your beautiful future!

VASALISA. The future frightens me.

BABA YAGA. Do not be frightened. She shall carry you to a new beginning in a new land. Ah, the firebird approaches. Come, we must find her! She awaits! She awaits!

(The **BABA YAGA** *pulls* **VASALISA** *off stage.)*

(Omaha. **DREW** *enters again.* **PEG** *senses he's back in the room and looks at him.)*

PEG. Yes?

DREW. You always say I put too much into the stage directions but at this point in the picture, I'd write, "Once in the kitchen, Drew opens the fridge and pauses for a moment, contemplating his new found freedom. Perhaps it's simply the bracing chill from the icebox, but he soon catches on to what really just happened. His mother has spun yet another tale."

PEG. *(trying to restrain her emotion)* Darling, it's not necessary to spell it all out.

(Chuckawalla. The mountains. **CONSTANCE** *and* **QUEENIE** *enter.)*

CONSTANCE. They'll never find us up here in the mountains. Why must you turn yourself in?

QUEENIE. Kid, you gotta know when it's time to surrender, only do it with flair.

(Omaha. We continue.)

DREW. The last words of the screenplay would be, "Drew returns to the parlor. He looks at his mother with an expression that somehow conveys amusement, grudging respect and above all, gratitude."

PEG. That's asking a lot of an actor.

(Chuckawalla. The mountains. **CONSTANCE** *takes* **QUEENIE**'*s hand.)*

CONSTANCE. I wish there was something more I could do.

QUEENIE. That feather on your hat. May I have that golden feather to take with me?

CONSTANCE. Of course.

(She removes the feather from her hat and gives it to **QUEENIE**.*)*

(Omaha. We continue.)

DREW. The only words he's able to say are "Thank you."

(Chuckawalla. The mountains. We continue.)

CONSTANCE. At least let me go with you.

QUEENIE. Honey, I've already gone. I've flown away on the wings of a giant bird. And no one can touch me.

(At the back of the stage, the golden firebird appears and on its back is a radiant **VASALISA**. *The caped and hooded figure of the* **BABA YAGA** *enters. We cannot see her face but we hear her echoed voice crying out exultantly.)*

BABA YAGA. Fly! My dear child! Fly!

End of Play

COSTUME PLOT

This play is about the power of imagination and so it's absolutely necessary that in many cases the actors must make instant transformations from character to character. Drew becomes Steve simply by adding a suit jacket and a fedora. Peg becomes Dr. Rutenspitz by adding a pair of glasses that perhaps hang from a chain around her neck. In Act Two, Queenie goes back and forth to being Queenie 2 with no change of costume at all. However, it works well for the Princess and Baba Yaga to be completely costumed and wigged. With the help of skilled dressers, there is ample time allotted for their changes.

ACT ONE

Scene One:
Peg – slightly dated 1940s suit, blouse, sensible shoes.
Drew – suit pants, shirt and tie, knit vest

Scene Two:
Drew adds suit jacket and Fedora as Steve
Queenie – full "new look" skirt, jacket, jabot, high heels
Verna – inappropriately flashy day dress, diamond necklace, bracelet and earrings, fur stole, blonde wig.

Scene Three:
Peg and Drew the same

Scene Three B:
Vasalisa – long flowing wig, Russian Princess dress, head dress.
Baba Yaga – ragged peasant dress, long flowing white wig.

Scene Three C:
Peg and Drew the same.

Scene Four:
Peg adds glasses as Dr. R.
Zygote – casual jacket and slacks and shirt, toupee.
Constance – lab coat, upswept wig

Scene Five:
Queenie – full skirt, elegant top, fur stole
Zygote the same as Scene four

Scene Six:
Queenie – same as Scene five
Constance – lab coat

Scene Seven:
Peg and Drew the same

Scene Eight:
Constance – severe ladies suit and blouse, simple hat
Drew adds jacket and fedora as Steve

Scene Nine:
Peg adds glasses as Dr. R

Scene Ten:
Steve wears jacket and fedora
Queenie – long flowing dressing gown
Zygote – gangster suit and hat
Verna – glamorous day suit

Scene Eleven:
Peg and Drew the same

Scene Twelve:
Peg adds glasses as Dr. R
Constance – lab coat
Steve wears jacket and fedora

Scene Thirteen:
Vasalisa the same as scene 1-3B
Baba Yaga adds voluminous flowing hooded cape to her 1-3B costume

Scene Fourteen:
Zygote the same as 1-10
Constance – lab coat

Scene Fifteen:
Peg and Drew the same
Queenie repeats look from 1-2
Zygote the same as 1-10
Verna – glamorous day suit
Peg adds glasses as Dr. R
Drew adds jacket and fedora as Steve
Queenie 2 – full costume change, same wig as Queenie 1, narrow skirt,
fitted top, spike heels, jewelry
Peg's overcoat

ACT TWO
Scene One:
Baba Yaga and Vasalisa same as 1-3B

Scene Two:
Peg and Drew the same as 1-15

Scene Three:
Constance – severe suit, blouse, loose hair

Scene Four:
Peg and Drew the same

Scene Five:
Queenie 2 – same costume as in 1-15
Verna – easy to remove coat/dress, 1940's foundation garments

Scene Six:
Queenie 2 becomes Queenie 1 with no change of costume.
Steve wears suit jacket and fedora

Scene Seven:
Queenie 1 becomes Queenie 2 with no change of costume.
Zygote – tuxedo

Scene Eight:
Steve wears jacket and fedora
Constance – suit and blouse from 2-3
Zygote – jacket, pants and shirt from 1-2

Scene Nine:
Peg and Drew the same

Scene Ten:
Queenie adds mink coat over Queenie 2 outfit
Drew adds suit jacket and fedora to become Steve
Constance – trench coat and hat with small yellow feather
Baba Yaga and Vasalisa same costumes as in 1-3B
The actor playing Zygote doubles for the Baba Yaga at the very end wearing the flowing hooded cape from 1-13

PROPS

ACT ONE
Scene One:
typewriter
Whiskey glass
Bottle of whiskey
Legal pad and pencil

Scene Two:
Tumbler of vodka – Queenie
Pistol

Scene Three:
None

Scene Three B:
Bladder of kvass
Baba Yaga's cane
Vasalisa's satchel with golden feather

Scene Three C:
None

Scene Four:
Clipboard
Syringe and vial of chemical

Scene Five:
Purse and cash
Zygote's drug case

Scene Six:
Queenie's purse, same as in previous scene

Scene Seven:
None

Scene Eight:
None

Scene Nine:
Legal pad and pencil (Peg's)

Scene Ten:
Letter from Constance

Scene Eleven:
Long data print out

Scene Twelve:
Package with bedroom slippers

Scene Thirteen:
Baba Yaga's cane

Scene Fourteen:
Keys to desk

Scene Fifteen:
Queenie's purse with cash
Zygote drug "works"
Magazine
Suitcase

ACT TWO
Scene One:
Baba Yaga's cane
Woven shawl

Scene Two:
None

Scene Three:
Schnapps bottle and glass

Scene Four:
None

Scene Five:
Gold lame gown
Bag with gun

Scene Six:
None

Scene Seven:
Same bag with gun from 2-5
Concert program

Scene Eight:
None

Scene Nine:
None

Scene Ten:
Queenie's gun set in mink coat pocket
Constance's gun
Baba Yaga cane